GIRONA
Banys Àrabs
Barri Vell
Catedral
Museu d'Art
Museu d'Arqueologia de Catalunya
Museu del Cinema
Museu dels Jueus
Passeig Arqueològic

LITORAL

TWINPACK
Costa Brava

MARY-ANN GALLAGHER

AA Publishing
If you have any comments or suggestions for this guide you can contact the editor at
travelguides@TheAA.com

How to Use This Book

KEY TO SYMBOLS

✚ Map reference

✉ Address

☎ Telephone number

🕐 Opening/closing times

🍴 Restaurant or café

🚆 Nearest rail station

🚌 Nearest bus route

⛴ Nearest riverboat or ferry stop

♿ Facilities for visitors with disabilities

? Other practical information

▷ Further information

ℹ Tourist information

✋ Admission charges: Expensive (over €8), Moderate (€4–€8), and Inexpensive (under €4)

★ Major Sight   ★ Minor Sight

👣 Walks   🚌 Drives

🏬 Shops

🎭 Entertainment and Activities

🍴 Restaurants

This guide is divided into four sections

• **Essential Costa Brava:** An introduction to the region and tips on making the most of your stay.

• **Costa Brava by Area:** We've broken the region into four areas, and recommended the best sights, shops, activities, restaurants, entertainment and nightlife venues in each one. Suggested walks and drives help you to explore.

• **Where to Stay:** The best hotels, whether you're looking for luxury, budget or something in between.

• **Need to Know:** The info you need to make your trip run smoothly, including getting about by public transport, weather tips, emergency phone numbers and useful websites.

Navigation In the Costa Brava by Area chapter, we've given each area its own colour, which is also used on the locator maps throughout the book and the map on the inside front cover.

Maps The fold-out map accompanying this book is a comprehensive map of the Costa Brava. The grid on this fold-out map is the same as the grid on the locator maps within the book. The grid references to these maps are shown with capital letters, for example A1. The grid references to the town plan are shown with lower-case letters, for example a1.

Contents

CONTENTS

Introducing the Costa Brava

The Costa Brava is a glorious stretch of coast, with plunging cliffs, turquoise coves and whitewashed fishing ports. Inland are medieval villages set amid vines and orchards, as well as the elegant little city of Girona, which preserves its medieval heart intact.

The Costa Brava stretches officially from Blanes to the French border, about 250km (155 miles) north. This was the first area of Spain to answer the siren call of mass tourism in the 1950s and 1960s, when sleepy fishing villages like Lloret de Mar were transformed almost overnight into high-rise resorts offering sun, sea and sand on a budget. There is still a smattering of resorts for cheerful package holidays, but the Costa Brava has gone decidedly upmarket in recent years. Chic boutique hotels and spa resorts have mushroomed across the region, and many visitors come for the wine and outstanding gastronomy. The revolution in Catalan cuisine has been under way for a couple of decades, and several of the finest restaurants in the world can be found here, including El Bulli (▷ 34 and 86), run by Ferran Adriá, and El Celler de Can Roca (▷ 34), with the Roca brothers at the helm.

Don't expect to hear much Spanish spoken, particularly inland. This is Catalonia, a proud nation with its own customs, traditions and language. Catalan is the official language of government, and widely spoken by locals—although along the cosmopolitan coast, which attracts people from around the world, you will hear a babel of tongues.

The gorgeous beaches and coves remain the biggest draw of the Costa Brava. They come in all shapes and sizes, from endless, golden sands to minuscule bays which are only accessible by coastal path or even by boat. There are fantastic facilities across the region for every kind of water sport, from sailing to kitesurfing, and the diving is outstanding, particularly in the marine reserves of Cap de Creus and the Illes Medes. Other popular activities include hiking, cycling and birdwatching (▷ 10–11).

Facts + Figures

- The Costa Brava is 256km (159 miles) long.
- It has an average of 300 days of sunshine a year.
- The Costa Brava celebrated its centenary in 2008.

BEACHES AND COVES

There are more than 100 beaches and coves along the Costa Brava, of which 29 have been awarded Blue Flag status, plus scores of spectacularly beautiful secret coves, which can be reached by the old smugglers' paths *(camins de ronda)*, or by boat.

FERRAN AGULLÓ

Ferran Agulló, writer, politician, poet and gourmet, coined the term 'Costa Brava' ('wild coast') in an article published in *La Veu de Catalunya (The Voice of Catalunya)* in 1908. According to some versions of the story, he was in Cala de Fornells, near Begur, when the term occurred to him. Others believe he uttered the words next to the lofty sanctuary of Sant Elm, near Sant Feliu de Guíxols.

THE *TRAMONTANA* WIND

The *tramontana* is a vicious, cold wind which whips across the northern Costa Brava and can last for several days at a time. The magnificent headland of the Cap de Creus stands testament to its fury, and has been stripped of almost all greenery by the wind. Dalí believed that it made the inhabitants of his home town of Figueres a little crazy—which, of course, he considered a good thing.

A Short Stay on the Costa Brava

DAY 1: GIRONA

Morning Start with a leisurely breakfast at one of the arcade cafés on the bustling Plaça de la Independència. Stroll down the lively Carrer de Santa Clara, lined with shops, and then cross the river at the Pont Pedra. This provides a wonderful vantage point to admire the Cases de l'Onyar, the multicoloured houses overhanging the River Onyar. Spend the morning getting lost in the atmospheric maze of Girona's historic old quarter. Visit the **Centre Bonastruc Ça Porta** (▷ 25) to learn about the Jewish community which flourished here in the Middle Ages, and go inside the magnificent **cathedral** (▷ 26), which has the world's widest nave.

Lunch Tuck into modern Catalan cuisine at **Occi** (▷ 34), a fashionable restaurant in the old quarter; it has a good set lunch menu on weekdays.

Afternoon Walk off lunch with a stroll along the **Passeig Arqueològic** (▷ 29), which curves around the old city and offers stunning views over the rooftops as far as the Pyrenees on a clear day. Then while away an hour or two amid the Romanesque frescoes and Gothic altarpieces in the **Museu d'Art** (▷ 27), set in a sumptuous medieval mansion.

Dinner Enjoy a glass of wine and perhaps some tapas on the terrace of the **Café Le Bistrot** (▷ 33), at the bottom of a grand flight of ancient stone steps. For a real treat, head to **El Celler de Can Roca** (▷ 34), regularly voted one of the best restaurants in the world. (You need to book months in advance for a table.) A less expensive option in the old town is **La Penyora** (▷ 34), a lively little spot serving interesting cuisine.

Later Check out the programme for the **Sunset Jazz Club** (▷ 32), and try and catch some live jazz.

DAY 2: CAP DE BEGUR

Morning Begin the day with a stroll around the fishing village of **Calella de Palafrugell** (▷ 41). Have breakfast in a seafront café and perhaps take a stroll along one of the old smugglers' paths *(camins de ronda)*, which lead to adjoining bays. Then jump in the car and drive to **Llafranc** (▷ 51) , the next cove along on the Cap de Begur.

Lunch Drive or walk up to the Far de Sant Sebastià, a graceful 19th-century lighthouse which still functions, and enjoy the views along the coast. The luxurious **Restaurante El Far** (▷ 62), next to the lighthouse, offers a weekday lunch menu for around €20. There are several less expensive choices in Llafranc, or you could even pick up some picnic supplies and enjoy them right on the beach.

Afternoon Spend the afternoon at the beach at **Tamariu** (▷ 54), enjoying the pine-clad cliffs and sandy bay. If you're feeling a bit more adventurous, rent a snorkel or book a dive, in order to fully appreciate the extraordinary natural beauty of this magnificent headland.

Early evening Head inland to the town of **Begur** (▷ 50). Wander through the narrow streets and climb up to the castle ruins, which offer amazing views over the plain and as far as the Pyrenees in clear weather.

Dinner There are plenty of dining options in Begur. **Dotze** (▷ 62) is a relaxed, fashionable spot with a terrace which offers delicious light meals. For something a little more traditional, try the **Fonda Caner** (▷ 62).

Later Several café-bars are clustered on the main square by the church in Begur. Order a glass of local wine and settle down to enjoy the spectacle of the crowds ebbing and flowing.

Top 25

These pages are a quick guide to the Top 25, which are described in more detail later. Here they are listed alphabetically, and the tinted background shows which area they are in.

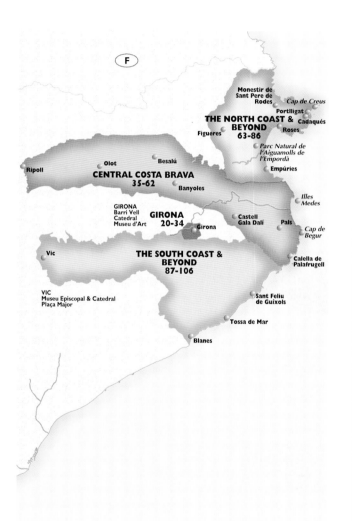

F

Monestir de
Sant Pere de
Rodes   Cap de Creus
                     Portlligat
THE NORTH COAST &   Cadaqués
        BEYOND   Roses
Figueres 63-86

        Besalú   Parc Natural de
Olot   l'Aiguamolls de
CENTRAL COSTA BRAVA   l'Empordà
Ripoll   35-62   Empúries
            Banyoles

                              Illes
                              Medes
GIRONA
Barri Vell   GIRONA   Castell
Catedral   20-34   Gala Dalí Pals
Museu d'Art   Girona   Cap de
                                  Begur
Vic   THE SOUTH COAST &
              BEYOND   Calella de
              87-106   Palafrugell

VIC
Museu Episcopal & Catedral
Plaça Major   Sant Feliu
                         de Guíxols

                Tossa de Mar

        Blanes

Out and About

The Costa Brava has four protected nature reserves, perfect for hiking and birdwatching, and the seaside resorts have facilities for every water sport, including snorkelling and diving. There are several excellent golf courses, as well as riding stables, and, further inland, companies can arrange balloon tours over the magnificent Catalan heartland. And if this sounds like too much work, you can always just lie back and relax on a gorgeous beach.

Birdwatching

The Costa Brava is a big destination for birdwatchers, particularly the wetlands of the Empordà (Aiguamolls de l'Empordà), which are now one of the most important refuges for waterbirds in Europe. Numerous rare bird species can also be found in the remote, craggy headland of the Cap de Creus.

Hiking

Two major European long-distance pathways converge on the Costa Brava: the trans-Pyrenean GR11, and the GR92, which skirts the Mediterranean coast (▷ 119). All the region's natural parks (▷ opposite) offer superb and well-signposted trails for hikers of all levels. The old coastal paths once used by smugglers *(camins de ronda)* have been restored in recent years, and are a fantastic way to explore the lesser-known tiny coves which pock the coastline.

FINDING PEACE AND QUIET

The seaside resorts may be packed in peak season, but it is easy to escape the crowds, particularly if you have your own transport. Even close to the coast, there are some alluring pockets of tranquillity. These include protected areas such as the little-known Muntanyes de Begur, with walks through woods and cliffs on the Cap de Begur, and the Massif de Montgrí, just behind Torroella de Montgrí. The hills of Les Gavarres are full of quiet picnic spots and are only a short drive from the coast.

From top: Heron in the Aiguamolls natural park; kayaks; walking in the Aiguamolls natural park

Cycling
Cycling in the Costa Brava is a very family-friendly activity, particularly in the flat plain of the lower Empordà. There is a network of centres (▷ 118) where you can rent bicycles and explore nearby biking trails.

Golf
There are several golf courses in the Costa Brava region, some of which enjoy a very high reputation. The regional tourist website, www.costabrava.org, has a comprehensive list.

Sailing and Water Sports
There are several dozen marinas, most with sailing schools, where you can try courses in everything from sailing to windsurfing. Diving and snorkelling are enormously popular along this rocky coast, particularly around the protected Illes Medes and Cap de Creus, and every resort has at least one company offering courses and equipment hire. The sandy beaches between Pals and Sant Pere Pescador are popular with windsurfers and kitesurfers.

Natural Parks
The beautiful wetlands of the Empordà were declared a nature reserve in 1983 to protect against encroaching development. This was the first of four natural parks and marine reserves created on the Costa Brava, which preserve pristine landscapes and give refuge to a wealth of terrestrial and aquatic flora and fauna. All provide outstanding opportunities for outdoor activities, particularly hiking and birdwatching.

From top: Getting ready to sail; having a round at Peralada Golf Club; kitesurfing

NATURAL PARKS AND MARINE RESERVES
There are are four natural parks and marine reserves in the Costa Brava region:
Parc Natural de l'Aiguamolls de l'Empordà (▷ 74–75)
Parc Natural de la Zona Volcànica de la Garrotxa (▷ 53)
Parc Natural de Cap de Creus (▷ 67)
Àrea Protegida de les Illes Medes i el Massif de Montgrí (▷ 44 and 55)

Shopping

Locally produced staples like wine and *embutits* (cured sausages), as well as specialities such as the hand-cured anchovies from L'Escala, should be high on any gourmet's shopping list. The region has also been famous for ceramics since the Middle Ages, particularly La Bisbal d'Empordà, where the streets are crammed with shops selling traditional crafts.

Wine
The wines of the Empordà region have become increasingly sophisticated in recent years. There are more than 40 wineries in the area and, although very few are open to visitors, their wines are readily available in shops in Girona and across the region. When choosing wines, note that the 2005 and 2007 vintages are particularly good.

Gourmet Treats
The market town of Vic (▷ 98) and the little country town of Castellfollit de la Roca (▷ 50) are both famous for their *embutits* (sausages). The most popular cured sausages are *fuet* and *llonganissa*, while *butifarra* is the classic cooked sausage, usually served with white beans. They are all readily available in shops and markets throughout the Costa Brava.

Ceramics
La Bisbal d'Empordà is the best place to find local pottery. As well as painted tiles and decorative tableware, there are also classic terracotta cooking dishes and water jars.

SALES
Sales (*rebaixes* in Catalan, *rebajas* in Spanish) are held twice a year in Spain, where prices are slashed by as much as 70 per cent. The best shopping in the Costa Brava region can be found in Girona, which is full of interesting fashion boutiques and quirky design stores. The winter sales start on 7 January, and the summer sales start on 1 July; both usually last for a month.

From top: Bottles of olive oil; ceramics at La Bisbal; Moscatel wine barrel; a typical butcher's shop

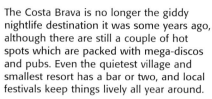

Costa Brava by Night

The Costa Brava is no longer the giddy nightlife destination it was some years ago, although there are still a couple of hot spots which are packed with mega-discos and pubs. Even the quietest village and smallest resort has a bar or two, and local festivals keep things lively all year around.

Nightclubs and Bars

Lloret de Mar is the most popular resort for nightlife. In summer, the centre throbs night and day with music, and the outskirts of town are crammed with mega-discos. Platja d'Aró is a little more upmarket, but is also packed with disco-bars, pubs and nightclubs. Girona is a lively university town, with plenty of midweek action, but at weekends and in summer when the students are absent, it is very quiet.

Local Scene

The local scene along the Costa Brava is much quieter than in the big resorts. Nightlife is centred around neighbourhood bars, which usually function as cafés during the day, then transform into bars as the night progresses.

Festivals

Every town and village has an annual festival in honour of its patron saint. These give visitors the chance to appreciate traditional Catalan customs, such as the stately *sardana* dance, the *correfoc* (fire-running) and processions of *gegants* (giants). For more on festivals, ▷ 114.

From top: Alfresco dining; night-time view of Girona; Malibu club and Marius bar in Platja d'Aro

---

MUSIC FESTIVALS

The Costa Brava hosts several spectacular festivals throughout the summer. The best include:

Festival dels Jardins de Cap Roig (www.caproig.cat)

Festival Internacional de Músiques de Torroella de Montgrí (www.festivaldetorroella.com)

Festival de Jazz Costa Brava, hosted in Palafrugell (www.palafrugell.cat)

Festival de Música de Begur (www.visitbegur.com)

Festival de Peralada (www.festivalperalada.com)

Eating Out

Catalan cuisine is based on seafood from the Mediterranean, fruit and vegetables from the plains, and meat and game from the hills. Thanks to top Catalan chefs at world-class restaurants, the Costa Brava has become popular with gourmet travellers.

Local Specialities
There are plenty of seafood specialities, such as *suquet*, a succulent fisherman's stew, traditionally prepared with monkfish and prawns, several Catalan versions of paella, including *fideuà*, made with tiny noodles instead of prawns, and *arròs negre* (black rice), made with squid ink. Other classic dishes are *canelones*, a version of cannelloni stuffed with meat or spinach, and *butifarra amb mongetes*, pork sausages with beans. Vegetable dishes include *escalivada*, made with roast aubergine, peppers and onions; *esqueixada*, a salad made with salted cod, tomatoes, peppers and olives; and *espinacs a la Catalana*, spinach tossed with olive oil, pine nuts and raisins.

Where to Eat
The traditional café-bar functions as a café by day and bar by night, and usually serves sandwiches, simple tapas and more substantial meals in an adjoining *comedor* (dining room). *Braseries*, or grills, are generally simple eateries serving fresh meat or fish, and *marisqueries* specialize in fish and shellfish. Restaurants run the gamut from small, family-run set-ups to fancy Michelin-starred restaurants.

EATING ON A BUDGET

Many restaurants, including the smartest and most upmarket, serve a fixed-price lunch menu *(menú del dia)* on weekdays. This is a great way to try the finest Catalan restaurants for a bargain price. The Costa Brava is also an ideal destination for picnics: pick up a loaf of fresh bread, some local cheeses and hams, and perhaps a bottle of local wine, and head down to the beach for a relaxed outdoor lunch.

The choice of restaurants and variety of cuisine is a highlight of any visit to the Costa Brava

Restaurants by Cuisine

There are restaurants to suit all tastes and budgets on the Costa Brava. On this page they are listed by cuisine. For detailed descriptions, see individual listings in Costa Brava by Area.

If You Like...

However you'd like to spend your time on the Costa Brava, these ideas should help you tailor your perfect visit. Each suggestion has a fuller write-up elsewhere in the book.

A LAZY MORNING

While away a morning at an outdoor café, such as Café del Parc, Girona (▷ 33).
Take a stroll around the charming medieval village of Pals (▷ 48).
Soak up the serenity at the monastery of Sant Joan de les Abadesses (▷ 54).
Visit the botanic gardens of Marimurtra, Blanes, high on a clifftop (▷ 90–91).
Gaze at the endless views from the bar terrace of Cap de Creus (▷ 85–86).

TASTY TAPAS

Try out the sophisticated tapas in Girona's old quarter at Boira (▷ 33).
Visit Divinum, Girona (▷ 34), a fashionable spot for creative tapas.
Sample traditional Galician-style tapas far from the crowds at La Tasqueta, Girona (▷ 34).
Enjoy simple tapas overlooking Begur's village square at Bar Es Castell (▷ 60).
Eat seafood tapas on the terrace of 1869, L'Escala (▷ 85), by the port.

There are many opportunities for taking a leisurely walk in town or along the coast (above)

Ceramics and pottery make ideal souvenirs (below)

QUIRKY GIFTS

Admire the unique, original jewellery using Girona's landmarks as inspiration at Ayuso Ramirez Joies, Girona (▷ 31).
Check out the treasure trove of antique objets d'art, including Modernista pieces, at Somnis, Girona (▷ 31).
Get your colourfully painted ceramics and kitchenware from Rulduà Ceràmica, La Bisbal d'Empordà (▷ 59).

Typical menu (right)

View of the Cap de Creus and one of its surreal rock shapes (below)

SEAFOOD BY THE SEA

Delight in astonishing sea views while dining on a clifftop terrace at the Restaurante El Far, Llafranc (▷ 62).
Enjoy the catch of the day on the terrace of Cal Nun, Cadaqués (▷ 85).
Try the classic fishermen's stew, *suquet*, at Es Baluard, Cadaqués (▷ 85), by the harbour.
Admire Mediterranean views over lunch at the elegant Villa Más, Sant Feliu de Guíxols (▷ 106).
Come to Rafa's, Roses (▷ 86), a legendary spot for the freshest fish.

THE GREAT OUTDOORS

Explore the hauntingly beautiful headland of Cap de Creus (▷ 67), with its remote coves and rugged hills.
Go diving in the beautiful marine reserve of Illes Medes, L'Estartit (▷ 44–45).
Take a hike through the volcanic landscape of the Parc Natural de la Zona Volcànica de la Garrotxa (▷ 53).
Visit the extensive wetlands of the Parc Natural de l'Aiguamolls de l'Empordà (▷ 74–75), an important waterbird refuge.

KEEPING THE KIDS HAPPY

Magic Park, Platja d'Aro (below)

Check out the earthquakes and volcanoes that accompany the pizzas at the unusual Disaster Café, Lloret de Mar (▷ 105–106).
Take the kids for waterskiing lessons with the Centre d'Esquí i Activitats Aquàtiques Ski-Bus, Begur (▷ 60).
Book a glass-bottomed boat trip with Dofijet Boats (▷ 104).
Visit one or more of the Costa Brava's water parks and theme parks (▷ 104).

AUTHENTIC FISHING VILLAGES

Spend the day in Calella de Palafrugell (▷ 41), whose whitewashed fishermen's cottages are clustered around a sandy bay.
Visit the chic little resort of Llafranc (▷ 51), which still preserves its traditional charm.
Explore the pretty harbour town of Tamariu (▷ 54–55), flanked by pine-clad cliffs.
Walk around the magical town of Cadaqués (▷ 66), backed by rugged hills and overlooking a pristine bay.
Discover the refreshingly low-key fishing harbour of El Port de la Selva (▷ 81) on the dramatic Cap de Creus headland.

View of Llafranc from the coastal path (below)

ROMANESQUE ART

Check out the magnificent Romanesque religious art in the Museu d'Art, Girona (▷ 27).
Appreciate the superb 12th-century sculpture of the Descent from the Cross at Sant Joan de les Abadesses (▷ 54).
Admire the carved monastery portal in Ripoll (▷ 49), one of the finest medieval artworks in Europe.
Learn about the fabulous horde of religious art acquired by the wealthy bishops of Vic at the Museu Episcopal, Vic (▷ 96–97).

Museu d'Art, Girona (above)

The west door of Ripoll's Santa Maria monastery (below)

PARTYING TILL DAWN

Enjoy the sounds at Platea, Girona (▷ 32), a sumptuous former theatre and now a popular club and music venue.
Be seen at the stylish Lux Café, Olot (▷ 60), which has DJs and regular live gigs.
Dance the night away at the enormous Discoteca Club & Loft (▷ 104), in the lively resort of Platja d'Aro.
Check out Disco Tropics (▷ 104), one of several mega-clubs in buzzy Lloret de Mar.

Assac Bar in Platja d'Aro (below)

Costa Brava by Area

GIRONA

CENTRAL COSTA BRAVA

THE NORTH COAST AND BEYOND

THE SOUTH COAST AND BEYOND

Girona is a beautiful, historic city piled up on the banks of the River Onyar, with an alluring old quarter crowned by a vast cathedral. Now a lively university town, it is crammed with excellent bars and shops and some outstanding restaurants.

Parc de la Devesa

EIXAMPLE

Plaça de la Independència

Museu del Cinema

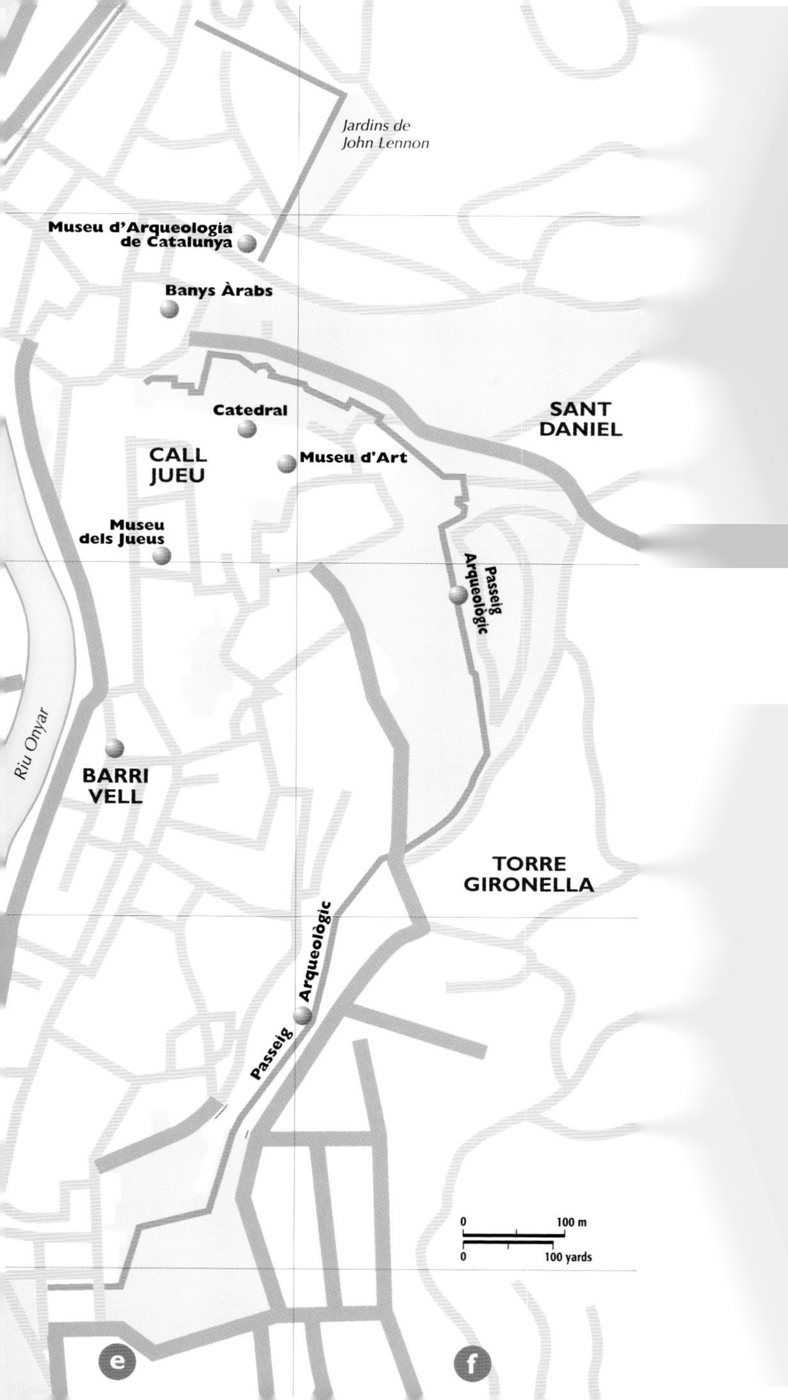

*Jardins de
John Lennon*

**Museu d'Arqueologia
de Catalunya**

Banys Àrabs

Catedral

**CALL
JUEU**

Museu d'Art

**SANT
DANIEL**

**Museu
dels Jueus**

Passeig
Arqueològic

Riu Onyar

**BARRI
VELL**

**TORRE
GIRONELLA**

Passeig Arqueològic

0		100 m
0		100 yards

e

f

Barri Vell

HIGHLIGHTS

● Les Cases de l'Onyar
● Rambla de la Llibertat
● Centre Bonastruc Ça Porta
● Museu d'Història de la Ciutat
● Banys Àrabs
● Archaeology museum
● Passeig Arqueològic

TIP

● The GironaMuseus Card offers discounted entry into the five municipal museums (pay for the first, then get 50 per cent off the others).

Girona's Barri Vell (Old Quarter) is a maze of narrow passages and squares, still partially ringed by ancient city walls. It has changed little over the centuries, although chic restaurants, shops and bars now occupy the secret courtyards.

Historic city The old city is piled up on a gentle hill next to the River Onyar, where a string of multicoloured houses (Les Cases de l'Onyar) are reflected in the waters. Running parallel to the river is the lively Rambla de la Llibertat, with smart shops and boutiques tucked into the graceful old arcades, and busy terrace cafés. Historic squares like the Plaça de l'Oli and the Plaça del Vi are named for the oil and wine markets once held here, and medieval guilds are recalled in the evocative street names, such

Clockwise from far left: Street in the Call Jueu; cafés near the Rambla; brightly painted houses overlooking the River Onyar; star detail in the cobblestones; the Pont de les Peixateries on the River Onyar

as Carrer Peixateries Velles (fishmongers) and Carrer de l'Argenteria (silversmiths).

Jewish quarter The oldest street in the Barri Vell is Carrer de la Força, which follows the line of the Roman road built 2,000 years ago and ends at the cathedral (▷ 26). It was once the main artery of the city's Jewish quarter, El Call. The Centre Bonastruc Ça Porta (▷ 29) tells the story of the city's Jewish community. Nearby, the Museu d'Història de la Ciutat occupies a 15th-century Gothic mansion, and offers an illuminating overview of the city's history. Beyond the old city gates are the Banys Àrabs (▷ 28) and the archaeology museum (▷ 28). There are fabulous views over the old city from the Passeig Arqueològic (▷ 29), a panoramic walkway.

THE BASICS

www.girona.cat/turisme

✚ e3

🛈 Carrer Joan Maragall 2, tel 872 975 975

♿ Few

❓ Guided tours of the city organized by tourist office and city history museum. See the website for more details

Catedral

Girona's cathedral, one of the great chuches of Spain and a triumph of architectural styles

THE BASICS

www.catedralgirona.org
🔹 e2
✉ Plaça de la Catedral
☎ 972 21 44 26
🕐 Apr–Oct daily 10–8; Nov–Mar Mon–Fri 10–7, Sat 10–4.30, Sun 2–8
🍴 Cafés nearby (€–€€€)
♿ Few
👆 Moderate
❓ Audioguides included in admission price

HIGHLIGHTS

● Nave
● Torre de Carlemany
● Chair of Charlemagne
● Cloister
● *Tapestry of the Creation*

TIP

● Look for La Bruixa de Pedra (the stone witch), a gargoyle on the Torre de Carlemany. According to legend she was a real witch who was turned to stone by God to stop her casting spells and curses.

Girona's magnificent cathedral, begun in 1312, dominates the old city. Its vast Gothic nave is the widest in the world (23m/75ft).

Monumental stairway The present cathedral replaced an earlier Romanesque church, of which little has survived except the lofty belltower called the Torre de Carlemany ('Charlemagne's Tower'). The visitor's entrance is reached via a grand rococo stairway, which sweeps up to a magnificent baroque facade.

Inside the cathedral The interior is resolutely Gothic, its enormous nave supported by soaring columns. Most of the stained glass, including the rose window, was inserted in the 18th century, although there are some beautiful fragments from the early 14th century. Off the nave is a series of chapels, and behind the main altar is a glimmering altarpiece, one of the loveliest creations of medieval religious silverwork. Behind a grille close to the main altar is the 11th-century Chair of Charlemagne, a bishop's throne of Pyrenean marble.

Cloister and museum The cloister galleries are lined with the tombs of long-gone Catalan nobles and bishops, and there are fine views of the Torre de Carlemany and its gargoyles. The museum contains some outstanding treasures, including a spectacular 11th-century *Tapestry of the Creation*, with its exquisitely embroidered depiction of the Garden of Eden.

TOP 25

Fine exhibits inside the Museum of Art (left); outside the museum (right)

Museu d'Art

The Palau Episcopal, formerly the bishop's grand residence, is round the corner from the cathedral and provides a fine setting for Girona's art collection.

Inside the palace The Episcopal Palace was built at the end of the 12th century and enlarged over subsequent centuries. It still has delicate Romanesque tracery around the windows, and a splendid Gothic stone staircase.

Artworks and curiosities The art collection is laid out chronologically, with the earliest galleries dedicated to Romanesque and pre-Romanesque artworks, including some delicate murals and a series of carved capitals from monasteries across the region. Look for the 12th-century *Christ In Majesty* and a delicate *Calvary* (13th century). The Gothic section is exceptionally good. The outstanding collection of paintings, sculpture and liturgical artefacts features a magnificent altarpiece by Lluís Borassà, from the monastery of Sant Miquel de Cruïlles (1416), and a gilded portrait of Santa Cristina by the Master of Olot. Later works include an altarpiece depicting devils prodding the damned into the mouth of hell at the Last Judgement. There are 19th-century landscapes from the School of Olot, and some early Modernista sculptures by Miquel Blay. Other curiosities are in galleries dedicated to furnishings, glassware and ceramics: look for the fascinating 17th-century printing press, one of the oldest in Spain.

THE BASICS

✚ e2
✉ Pujada de la Catedral 12
☎ 972 20 38 34
🕐 Mar–Sep Tue–Sat 10–7, Sun 10–2; Oct–Feb Tue–Sat 10–6, Sun 10–2
🍴 Several cafés nearby (€–€€€)
♿ Good
✋ Inexpensive

HIGHLIGHTS

● *Christ In Majesty*
● *Calvary*
● Altarpiece (1416)
● Portrait of Santa Cristina
● Modernista sculptures by Miquel Blay
● Printing press

TIP

● If it's open, peek into the Farmàcia Santa Caterina, which has been reconstructed within the museum and is lined with antique blue-and-white pots. It is said to be the oldest pharmacy in the city.

GIRONA ★ TOP 25

More to See

BANYS ÀRABS

www.banysarabs.cat

These beautiful 12th-century baths are a recreation of the North African Islamic style of bathhouses, with their delicate horseshoe arches and slender columns. There are five rooms within the complex, but the highlight is the dressing area, which is subtly lit by a pierced stone cupola. The baths are regularly used as a temporary exhibition space.

✚ e2 ✉ Carrer Ferrán el Catòlic s/n ☎ 972 21 32 62 🕓 Apr–Sep Mon–Sat 10–7, Sun 10–2; Oct–Mar daily 10–2 🍴 Plenty of cafés nearby (€–€€) ♿ Few ✋ Inexpensive (free last Sun of the month)

MUSEU D'ARQUEOLOGIA DE CATALUNYA

www.mac.cat

The archaeology museum is set in a huge Romanesque monastery. Its artefacts are displayed in the echoing nave and around the lovely cloister. Among the finds on show are palaeolithic tools, painted vases from the earliest Greek settlers, richly sculpted Roman sepulchres and vibrant mosaics. It is currently being remodelled, so some sections may be closed to visitors.

✚ e2 ✉ Carrer Santa Llúcia 8 🕓 Jun–Sep Tue–Sat 10.30–1.30, 4–7, Sun 10–2.30; Oct–May Tue–Sat 10–2, 4–6, Sun 10–2.30 🍴 Plenty of cafés nearby (€–€€) ♿ Few ✋ Inexpensive (free last Sun of the month)

MUSEU DEL CINEMA

www.museudelcinema.org

This museum explores cinema from its earliest beginnings to the arrival of television. Cinema buffs will be fascinated by the exhibits, which include descriptions of ancient Japanese optical tricks used 2,000 years ago to projections of the earliest moving pictures. There's a small shop, perfect for offbeat gifts for cinephiles.

✚ d4 ✉ Carrer Sèquia 1 ☎ 972 41 27 77 🕓 May–Sep Tue–Sun 10–8; Oct–Apr Tue–Fri 10–6, Sat 10–8, Sun 11–3. Guided visits in summer Tue–Sun at 12pm and 6pm; in winter Sat 6pm, Sun 12pm 🍴 Plenty of cafés nearby (€–€€) ♿ Very good ✋ Moderate

The octagonal pool in the Banys Àrabs

Sant Pere de Galligants houses the archaeology museum

MUSEU DELS JUEUS

At its peak, during the 13th century, Girona's Jewish community numbered a thousand, and the city was famous throughout Europe as a centre of learning and culture. The Jewish quarter, known as El Call, passed into Christian hands after the expulsion of the Jews in 1492, and its most important ritual buildings were destroyed. However, the Centre Bonastruc Ça Porta (named for a celebrated Jewish philosopher) was established in 1997 over what is believed to be the ruins of a 15th-century synagogue. It contains a fascinating little museum dedicated to the history of the Jews of Catalonia, with medieval costumes (chillingly adorned with the identifying badges which Jews were required to wear), reproductions of the ritual baths (mikveh), and descriptions of some of the most notable Jewish figures of the period.

➕ e2 ✉ Carrer de la Força 8 ☎ 972 21 57 61 🕐 Jul–Aug Mon–Sat 10–8, Sun 10–2; Sep–Jun Mon 10–2, Tue–Sat 10–6, Sun 11–2 🍴 Numerous cafés and restaurants nearby (€–€€€) ♿ Good ✋ Inexpensive (free first Sun of the month)

PASSEIG ARQUEOLÒGIC

www.girona.cat

A spectacular walking path, called the Passeig de la Muralla or Passeig Arqueòlogic, has been created on top of the thick walls that circle much of the eastern swathe of the old city. The earliest sections of these walls are Carolingian, and date back to the ninth century, although much of it was built between the 14th and 15th centuries. The Torre Gironella is where the Jews hid during the pogrom of 1391. The views are spectacular, reaching out across the rooftops to the mountains beyond the city.

➕ e2–e5 ✉ Access from several points, including from the Jardins de John Lennon, just behind the archaeology museum 🕐 Always open 🍴 Plenty of cafés nearby (€–€€) ♿ None

Detail on the facade of the Museu del Cinema

Part of the walkway along the medieval ramparts of the city

A Walk Around the Old Quarter

This walk is an introduction to Girona's atmospheric old quarter, taking in some of its most important monuments.

DISTANCE: 2km (1.2 miles) **ALLOW:** 2–5 hours, depending on stops

START

PLAÇA DE LA INDEPENDÈNCIA
🗺 e3

END

PLAÇA DE LA INDEPENDÈNCIA

GIRONA · **WALK**

1 Start on Plaça de la Independència, packed with cafés and restaurants. Take the Pont de Sant Agustí, pausing to admire the colourful houses, to plunge into the heart of the Barri Vell.

2 Take the first street on your left, Carrer Ballesteries, and follow it to the church of Sant Feliu. It contains the relics of Girona's patron saint, Sant Narcís, in a small chapel.

3 Pass through Portal Sobreportes, a medieval gateway, which leads into Plaça de la Catedral. From here, a rococo staircase sweeps majestically up to the superb cathedral (▷ 26).

4 Adjoining the cathedral is the Gothic bishop's palace, containing the Museu d'Art (▷ 27).

8 Cross Carrer de la Força to return to the Pont de Sant Agustí and Plaça de la Independència.

7 The steps end in Carrer de la Força, once the main street of Girona's medieval Jewish ghetto. On the right is Centre Bonastruc Ça Porta (▷ 25).

6 A flight of steps, Pujada de Sant Domènec, leads past some of the city's finest Gothic and Renaissance palaces, including Palau Caramany.

5 From the museum, take Carrer Belmirall, turning briefly left onto Carrer Alemanys to reach Plaça Sant Domènec, flanked by the 16th-century rectory of Girona University and a 13th-century convent.

Shopping

50CL
www.vinoteca50cl.cat
This new wine shop, in an old town house in the Barri Vell, specializes in Catalan wines, particularly those of the Empordà region near the city, although you'll find a well-chosen selection from other parts of Spain.
🔆 e3 ✉ Plaça de les Castanyes 10 ☎ 972 48 39 38

AYUSO RAMIREZ JOIES
www.ayusoramirez.es
The striking, contemporary jewellery here includes bracelets, earrings and necklaces, which take their inspiration from the silhouettes of famous Girona landmarks, such as the cathedral and the church of Sant Narcís.
🔆 e4 ✉ Plaça de Catalunya 7 ☎ 972 20 40 43

EL CORTÉ INGLES
www.elcorteingles.es
Spain's biggest department store has a branch in Girona. It is the perfect one-stop shop, with everything from fashion (for men, women and children) to electrical goods, a restaurant and supermarket.
🔆 Off map at c5 ✉ Carrer Barcelona 106–110 ☎ 972 18 84 00

ETXART & PANNO
www.etxartpanno.com
Catalan designer Emi Panno creates eye-catching, contemporary fashion and accessories for women at prices which won't break the bank. It includes fabulous silk maxi dresses with bold designs.
🔆 e3 ✉ Carrer Santa Clara 25 ☎ 972 48 50 14

FREIXA
Freixa stocks shoes for men, women and children, including gorgeous footwear for women designed by the likes of Dorotea and Pura Lopez. There are bags and belts too.
🔆 e3 ✉ Carrer Santa Clara 41 ☎ 972 21 48 48

LLIBRERÍA LES VOLTES
This atmospheric bookshop was first established in the 1960s to encourage the sale of books in Catalan, banned under the Dictatorship. It remains fiercely

nationalist, and offers a range of books on Girona and Catalonia, as well as gift items bearing the Catalan flag.
🔆 e4 ✉ Plaça del Vi 2 ☎ 972 20 19 69

NECTAR
Cakes, chocolates and all kind of delicious goodies are available at this *pastisseria*, where you'll find Catalan specialities such as *bunyols* (little doughnuts stuffed with cream or chocolate, available at Easter) and *panellets* (marzipan sweets rolled in pine nuts, typically eaten around All Saints').
🔆 d3 ✉ Carrer Nord 22 ☎ 972 42 74 10

EL PETIT PARADÍS
This wonderful gourmet shop and deli in the centre of town has a fabulous range of local, national and international wines, cheeses, hams and oils, which are great for picnics or gifts.
🔆 c4 ✉ Travesía del Carril 1 ☎ 972 21 59 25

SOMNIS
It's easy to be tempted by the beautiful armoires and cabinets at this antiques store, but if you're looking for a special souvenir that will fit in the suitcase, take a look at the Modernista vases, vintage jewellery and photograph frames.
🔆 e3 ✉ Carrer Mercaders 6 ☎ 972 21 34 94

GIRONA

SHOPPING

Entertainment and Activities

L'ARC

This mellow café-bar has a fabulous terrace at the base of the huge flight of steps leading up to the cathedral. Inside, the vaulted space is crammed with posters. There are regular art exhibitions and occasionally someone sits down at the battered piano and starts singing.
✚ e2 ✉ Plaça de la Catedral 9 ☎ 972 20 30 87 🕓 May–Sep Sun, Wed 10am–1am, Thu–Sat 10am–2am; Oct–Apr, Sun, Tue, Wed 11am–midnight, Thu–Sat 11am–2am

EL MUSEU DEL VI

www.elmuseu.com
During the day and early evening this café-bar is popular for its abundant and well-priced tapas, sandwiches and *racions*, but as the night progresses it becomes more of a place to hang out. It's popular with students, and the absinthe *xupitos* ('shots') are legendary.
✚ e2 ✉ Carrer Cort Reial 4 ☎ 972 21 34 85 🕓 Daily 9am–2am

LA PLACETA

This is one of the few places in Girona where you can listen to rock music. DJs keep the crowd happy with every-thing from Jimi Hendrix to nu-metal and heavy.
✚ e3 ✉ Carrer Bonaventura Carreras i Peralta 7 ☎ 972 22 02 18 🕓 May–Sep Mon–Sat

6pm–3am; Oct–Apr Thu–Sat 10pm–3am

PLATEA

Chandeliers drip from the ceiling of this opulent old theatre, now a fashionable music bar. As well as the regular DJ sessions, it hosts live acts. The admission charge (€10) includes a drink.
✚ d2 ✉ Carrer Jeroni Real de Fontclara 4 ☎ 972 22 72 88 🕓 Closed Sun–Tue and Jul–Aug

SALA LA PLANETA

www.laplaneta.net
This small, independent theatre hosts a wide-ranging programme of theatre, music, readings and special events for children. Check the website for full details.
✚ e3 ✉ Passeig Canalejas 3 ☎ 972 20 77 54

SUNSET JAZZ CLUB

www.sunsetjazz-club.com
The low-lit, stone-vaulted Sunset Jazz Club is open every day, but concerts

PARTY NIGHT

Girona may be Catalonia's second-largest city (after Barcelona), but the nightlife scene is surprisingly quiet and low-key, partly because Girona is a university city, and most students return home to their families on Fridays. The best night to go out is Thursday, when the students let off steam before returning to their villages the next day.

are generally held on Thursdays, Saturdays and Sundays. It's a great place to hang out even when there isn't a concert; its walls are papered with paintings and photographs, and there's a relaxed, candle-lit atmosphere. Check the website for details.
✚ e1 ✉ Carrer Jaume Pons i Martí 12 ☎ 872 08 01 45 🕓 Daily 8pm–late

TEATRE MUNICIPAL

www.girona.cat/teatremunicipal
The city's elegant 19th-century theatre, in the heart of the Barri Vell, has an excellent programme of drama, contemporary dance, music and even screen opera (there's a live link with Barcelona's prestigious Liceu opera house).
✚ e4 ✉ Plaça del Vi 1 ☎ 972 41 90 18

VOLS ROSELL

http://volsrosell.com
This company offers unforgettable balloon flights over the glorious hills of Les Gavarres and the Empordà region, which depart from the Parc de la Devesa in the centre of Girona. Flights usually take between 90 minutes and 2 hours and costs around €160, including a country breakfast of cured meats.
✚ c2 ✉ Parc de la Devesa, La Copa ☎ 972 20 62 91, 659 936 203

Restaurants

ALBEREDA (€€€)

www.restaurantalbereda.com

The Albereda is justly considered to be one of Girona's finest restaurants. The sophisticated cuisine has Mediterreanean roots, but occasionally strays around the globe: the prized local Palamós prawns, served with their juice and trout caviar, appear on the menu next to tuna tataki with fennel, soya and cocoa.

➕ e4   ✉ Carrer Albereda 7   ☎ 972 22 60 02   ⏰ Lunch and dinner; closed Mon dinner, public hols

ARTS CAFÉ (€–€€)

This popular café on Rambla de la Llibertat has a great terrace for watching the world go by. It serves excellent sandwiches (try the goat's cheese with *escalivada*, a Catalan salad made with roast peppers, onions and aubergines), as well as crêpes, salads and ice cream. It's a good option for an easy lunch with kids, or if you are hungry outside normal restaurant hours.

➕ e3   ✉ Rambla de la Llibertat 7   ☎ 972 22 70 84   ⏰ Daily lunch and dinner

BAU BAR (€€)

www.baubargirona.com

Bau Bar has a wide-ranging menu of Catalan and Mediterranean dishes, but it can also provide (with prior notice) a menu featuring Sephardic Jewish cuisine.

➕ e2   ✉ Plaça de la Catedral 8   ☎ 972 48 50 07   ⏰ Daily lunch and dinner

BOIRA (€–€€)

Boira has a terrace on the arcaded Plaça de la Independència, a downstairs bar area serving tapas, and an elegant dining room upstairs with views over the Cases de l'Onyar (▷ 24). It serves modern Mediterranean and Catalan cuisine at reasonable prices, along with a decent wine list.

➕ e3   ✉ Plaça de la Independència   ☎ 972 49 04 87   ⏰ Daily lunch and dinner

CAFÉ LE BISTROT (€)

Le Bistrot offers simple dishes like Catalan *canelones* (cannelloni stuffed with spinach or meat and topped with béchamel sauce), and home-made 'pizzas', which are actually huge slices of toasted country bread with a range of toppings. There are also platters of locals hams and cheeses. It fills up quickly, so come early.

➕ f3   ✉ Pujada Sant Domènec 7   ☎ 972 21 88 03   ⏰ Daily lunch and dinner

CAFÉ DEL PARC (€)

This sweet café is in the Parc del Migdia. It serves delicious home-made pastries for breakfast, and the buffet lunch includes a surprisingly good range of vegetarian dishes.

➕ Off map at e5   ✉ Carrer Pau Vila 1   ☎ 972 20 24 14   ⏰ Daily lunch and dinner

CAL ROS (€€€)

www.calros-restaurant.com

Cal Ros prides itself on its market-fresh Catalan dishes prepared according to traditional recipes with a contemporary twist. The owners source their ingredients locally, and serve organic produce where possible. House specialities include *arròs a la cassola*, a rice casserole cooked in an iron pot.

➕ e2   ✉ Carrer Cort Reial 9   ☎ 972 21 91 76   ⏰ Lunch and dinner; closed Sun dinner, Mon

GIRONA

RESTAURANTS

CASA MARIETA (€€)

It might look a bit like a tourist trap from the outside, but it serves great Catalan cuisine. There's a good choice of dishes, from *l'anèc amb peres* (duck with pears) to *suquet de peix* (Catalan fish stew), and a bargain *menú del día* on weekday lunchtimes.
➕ e3 ✉ Plaça de la Independència 5–6 ☎ 972 20 10 16 🕐 Lunch and dinner; closed Mon

EL CELLER DE CAN ROCA (€€€)

This is regularly voted one of the best restaurants in the world, and the Roca brothers have won countless awards for their magnificent cuisine. It's a mecca for gourmets, so book well in advance for what is the dining experience of a lifetime.
➕ Off map at a1 ✉ Can Sunyer 48 ☎ 972 22 67 83 🕐 Lunch and dinner; closed Sun, Mon

DIVINUM (€€)

www.divinum.cat
Divinum offers a range of tapas, as well as more substantial dishes. There are classics like lamb chops with chickpeas or duck breast with cherries, along with more unusual fare such as squid stuffed with spinach, ceps and shiitake mushrooms.
➕ e3 ✉ Carrer General Fournàs 2 ☎ 872 08 02 18 🕐 Lunch and dinner; closed Mon

LA FORÇA VELLA (€€)

La Força Vella specializes in traditional country cooking, such as *conill* (rabbit) and *cargols* (snails), and good paella and other rice dishes, and the fixed-price lunch menu is a good deal.
➕ e3 ✉ Carrer de la Força 4 ☎ 972 22 72 02 🕐 Lunch and dinner; closed Mon

KIWI (€)

Kiwi offers light, tasty cakes and snacks and a good fixed-price lunch menu. It has art exhibitions and mellow music in the background, and is an enjoyable place for a break.
➕ e3 ✉ Carrer Mercaders 13 ☎ 972 20 63 14 🕐 Daily lunch and dinner

OCCI (€€€)

www.restaurantocci.com
Occi serves imaginative, exquisitely presented Mediterranean cuisine. Unusual dishes include a delicate prawn carpaccio, as well as more traditional fare such as *bacallà a la llauna* (oven-baked cod).
➕ e3 ✉ Carrer Mercaders 4 ☎ 972 22 71 54 🕐 Lunch and dinner; closed Sun, Mon

LA PENYORA (€€)

The menu at La Penyora includes tasty dishes such as courgette flowers stuffed with cheese and vegetables, and Catalan *canelones* with wild mushrooms and pork.
➕ e4 ✉ Carrer Nou del Teatre ☎ 972 21 89 48 🕐 Lunch and dinner; closed Sun dinner, Tue

LA POMA (€€)

La Poma serves creative tapas and light meals, including *croquetas* with wild mushrooms, imaginative salads and sandwiches (try the roast beef with onion marmalade). Reservations recommended.
➕ e2 ✉ Carrer Cort Reial 13 ☎ 972 21 29 09 🕐 Lunch and dinner; closed Tue

LA TASQUETA (€)

This old-fashioned restaurant serves typical Galician tapas and a hearty fixed-price lunch menu at bargain prices. Try the *pulpo a la gallega*, succulent octopus lightly flavoured with paprika, or the local anchovies from L'Escala.
➕ Off map at b5 ✉ Avinguda Sant Narcís 65 ☎ 972 40 71 20 🕐 Lunch and dinner; closed Sun

---

MICHELIN STARS

Chef Joan Roca, of Girona's celebrated restaurant El Celler de Can Roca (▷ above), received his third Michelin star in 2010, bringing the total number of three-star restaurants in Spain to seven. Four of these are in Catalonia: El Celler de Can Roca, El Bullí in Roses, Can Fabes in Sant Celoni and Sant Pau in Sant Pol de Mar.

This chapter covers the wild coast around Begur, with its coves and whitewashed fishing villages, as well as the golden, medieval villages of the inland plain. It also stretches inland to the historic Catalan heartland around Olot and Ripoll.

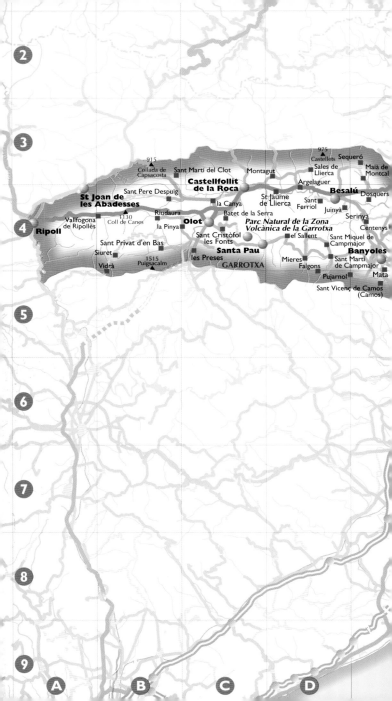

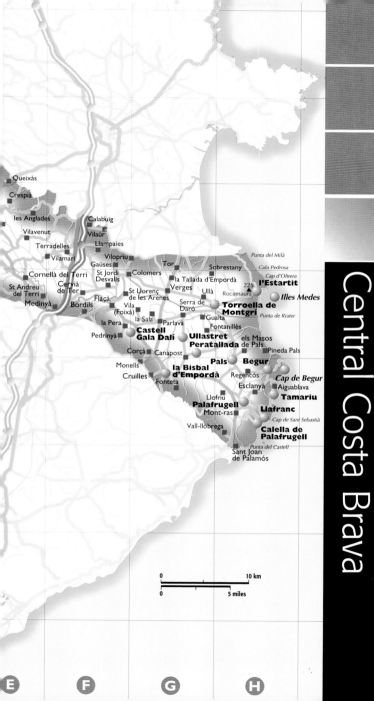

Queixàs

Crespià

les Anglades

Vilavenut

Calabuig

Terradelles

Vilaür

Vilamarí

Llampaies

Vilopr
Gaüses

St Jordi
Desvalls

Tor

Sobrestany

Cornellà del Terri

Colomers

la Tallada d'Empordà

St Andreu
del Terri

Cervià
de Ter

St Llorenç
de les Arenes

Verges

Ullà

**Torroella de
Montgrí**

Medinyà

Flaçà

Vila
(Foixà)

Serra de
Daró

la Pera

la Sala

Parlavà

Gualta

Fontanilles

Bòrdils

Pedrinyà

**Castell
Gala Dalí**

**Ullastret
Peratallada**

els Masos
de Pals

Corçà

Canapost

Pals

Begur

Monells

**la Bisbal
d'Empordà**

Regencós

Cap de Begur

Cruïlles

Fonteta

Esclanyà

Aiguablava

Llofriu

Palafrugell

Tamariu

Mont-ras

Llafranc

Vall-llobrega

Cap de Sant Sebastià

**Calella de
Palafrugell**

Punta del Castell

Sant Joan
de Palamós

Punta del Milà

Cala Pedrosa

Cap d'Olrera

l'Estartit

Rocamaura

225 ▲

Illes Medes

Punta de Riuter

0   10 km

0   5 miles

Central Costa Brava

E   F   G   H

Banyoles

TOP 25

HIGHLIGHTS

- Plaça Major
- Museu Darder
- Monestir de Sant Esteve
- A boat ride across the lake
- Swimming in the lake

TIP

- The tourist office can arrange free guided visits of the old town and the lake, including family-friendly activities. Most are in Catalan or Spanish, but some guides speak English and other languages.

Banyoles grew up around a ninth-century monastery and preserves an appealing old quarter, but its biggest draw is the vast lake, fringed with forest and dotted with miniature Modernista fishing cabins.

Historic centre The old quarter of Banyoles, the Casc Antic, is tiny, with just a handful of narrow streets leading off the Plaça Major. Laid out in the 13th century, the square is still trimmed with stone porticoes, which provide shade for terrace cafés and the Wednesday morning market. The Museu Darder has five floors of artefacts, including finds from the oldest neolithic settlement on the Iberian peninsula, just outside Banyoles. The old town grew up in the shadow of the Monestir de Sant Esteve, the first Benedictine monastery in Catalonia. The

Clockwise from far left: The Romanesque Church of Santa Maria near Estany de Banyoles; Pesquera Marimon—a typical fisherman's house by the lake; taking a stroll along the lakeshore; shops and arcades in Plaça Major; rowing boats on the lake; Banyoles' main square has great dining opportunities

present building is an 11th-century replacement of the original ninth-century edifice, but the cloister contains fragments from the early pre-Romanesque church.

Banyoles Lake Most people come to Banyoles to admire its serene lake, Estany de Banyoles, the largest in Catalonia. It has been a popular summer resort since the mid-19th century, when fishermen began to build the fanciful little Modernista fishing pavilions, called *pesqueres*, on the lakeshore. You can cruise the lake on a sailing boat, rent a kayak or take a dip in one of the natural bathing areas. Paths—good for hiking, biking and horse-riding—meander through the forests around the lake. One of the best leads to the attractive stone village of Porqueres, on the western shores of the lake.

THE BASICS

www.banyoles.cat
(Catalan only)
➕ E4
ℹ️ Passeig Darder, pesquera No. 10, tel 972 58 34 70
🚆 Train or bus to Girona, then TEISA bus to Banyoles
♿ Good

Besalú

The medieval Pont Vell (left and right); the Church of Sant Pere (middle)

THE BASICS

www.besalu.cat

🕀 D4

ℹ Plaça de la Llibertat 1, tel 972 59 12 40

🚌 To Girona or Figueres, then TEISA bus to Besalú

♿ Few

❓ Guided visits are offered by the tourist office (usually in Spanish and Catalan, although other languages are available during the peak summer season). A miniature train tours the town in summer

HIGHLIGHTS

● Pont Vell and Plaça Major
● Churches of Sant Pere and Sant Vicenç
● Centre d'Interpretació del Patrimoni Jueu (Jewish Heritage Interpretation Centre)

TIP

● Besalú is very popular with coach parties: if possible, avoid weekends, and try to stay the night to enjoy it when the crowds leave.

Besalú is a perfect little time-capsule of a medieval town, complete with a picturesque Romanesque bridge spanning the River Fluvià. Its elegant mansions, arcaded streets and handsome churches are testament to its historic importance.

History Besalú is crowned by the sparse remnants of a castle. The rest of the town has fared considerably better, and the huddle of mansions, churches and courtyards is so picturesque that it resembles a film set. It is most famous for its medieval bridge, the Pont Vell, built in the 12th century and remodelled in 1315, which spans the River Fluvià in seven graceful arches.

Old city The best way to appreciate Besalú is to wander its cobbled streets, or soak up the enchanting surroundings over a glass of wine. There are plenty of cafés and traditional inns on Plaça Major, the heart of the town. The finest surviving church is Sant Pere, consecrated in 1003, which features some fabulous Romanesque sculptures of lions and leering monkeys around the portal and windows. The even earlier church of Sant Vicenç has a charming facade festooned with stone garlands. Perhaps most remarkable are the remnants of the Mikve, the only surviving ritual Jewish bathhouse on the Iberian peninsula. Between the 13th and 15th centuries, about a quarter of the population was Jewish: their story is told in an interpretation centre on the Plaça dels Jueus.

The pleasant resort of Calella de Palafrugell has lost nothing of its original charm

Calella de Palafrugell

The whitewashed fishing village of Calella de Palafrugell oozes old-fashioned charm. Tourism has long replaced fishing as the main industry, but the local sailors are still recalled in the *havaneres*, traditional sea shanties.

Ports and beaches The lanes around the port are lined with old fishermen's cottages, painted brilliant white. Families gather to enjoy superb seafood at the beachfront restaurants, whose shady terraces overlook the sea. Steps and passages link miniature squares and offer tantalizing glimpses of the bay. A coastal path winds along the seafront, linking the village with Llafranc (▷ 51), and passing a handful of breathtaking coves. The beaches are small along this rugged coast, but their turquoise waters and pine-clad cliffs are enchanting.

Havaneres Every summer, thousands of musicians gather on the main beach for the *Cantada de Havaneres*. They sing plaintive sea shanties, first brought back from Cuba by Catalan sailors during the 19th century. The traditional accompaniment is *cremat*, coffee spiced with cinnamon and rum, served flambéed in a terracotta dish.

Botanic garden Just south of the village is the Jardí Botànic de Cap Roig, a magnificent garden which was laid out in 1927. With its stunning cliff-top setting, it is considered one of the finest gardens in the Mediterranean.

THE BASICS

www.visitpalafrugell.cat

✚ H6

🛈 Carrer de les Voltes 6, tel 972 61 44 75

🚌 SARFA or TEISA buses from Girona and Figueres

♿ Few

Jardí Botànic de Cap Roig

http://jardins.caproig.cat

🕐 Mon–Fri 10–8 (until 6pm in winter), Sat–Sun 10–6; Jan–Feb Sat–Sun only

💰 Moderate

HIGHLIGHTS

● Old town around the port
● Seafood dinner overlooking the beach of Port Bo
● Cliff walk to Llafranc
● Jardí Botànic de Cap Roig

TIP

● There are few hotels in Calella de Palafrugell, so book in advance. It's slightly easier to find apartments and villas for rent.

Cap de Begur

The turquoise bay of Cap Aiguablava (left); beach at the resort of Fornells (right)

THE BASICS

www.visitbegur.com

H6

Avinguda Onze de Setembre 5, tel 972 62 45 20

SARFA bus from Girona and Figueres to Begur, then local bus or taxi to the resorts

Few

HIGHLIGHTS

● Exploring the *camins de ronda*, breathtaking coastal paths
● Snorkelling in the translucent waters
● Trying the local speciality, *peix de roca* (rock fish), traditionally cooked in a *suquet* (a Catalan fish stew)

TIP

● The rocky Muntanyes de Begur are very little known, and the hiking paths through these mountains are relatively quiet, even in the height of summer.

The Cap de Begur encapsulates all the magic of the Costa Brava: steep cliffs plunging to perfect bays, whitewashed villages, and pine-scented Mediterranean forest criss-crossed with walking paths.

Pristine coastline Although the region has long been discovered by tourists, it has remained gloriously unspoilt. This pristine beauty comes at a price, however: the highly sought-after properties are among the most expensive anywhere in Spain. Despite the relative lack of hotels, the region remains enormously popular with Catalan families.

Picturesque resorts The small resorts strung along the coastline are linked by coastal paths (*camins de ronda*), cut into the reddish rock and once used by fishermen and sailors. To the south, Aiguablava is the largest bay, surrounded by elegant villas and dominated by a modern *parador* atop a cliff. A rocky path links it to more stunning coves and beaches, particularly those at Fornells, where, in 1908, local journalist Ferran Agulló first coined the term 'costa brava'. Another path winds between Sa Tuna, regularly voted the prettiest resort of the Costa Brava, and Aiguafreda. A superb walking path heads inland from the coast to Begur (▷ 50), and a section of the 580km (360-mile) long GR92 hiking trail crosses the Muntanyes de Begur (a craggy nature reserve) and offers panoramic views over the entire Gulf of Roses. There are also excellent opportunities for water sports.

The castle at Púbol became a shrine to the memory of Dalí's wife, Gala

Castell Gala Dalí

This 11th-century castle, complete with fairy-tale towers and crenellations, was bought by Salvador Dalí in 1969 as a gift for his beloved wife and muse, Gala, who held court here until her death in 1982.

Story of a muse Gala was born in Russia in 1894. She married French poet Paul Éluard in 1917, but left him for Dalí in 1929, and became his muse for the rest of her life. The castle was virtually in ruins when it was purchased by Dalí, who had it rebuilt in a typically surreal mixture of the sublime and the grotesque.

Interiors and garden In 1996, the castle was opened as a museum and forms the third part of the so-called Dalí Triangle, along with the Teatre-Museu Dalí in Figueres (▷ 70–71), and the Casa-Museu Salvador Dalí, in Portlligat, (▷ 76). The interior furnishings are surprisingly restrained, even austere. The grandest salon is the Coat-of-Arms Room, in which Dalí placed a throne for Gala and painted the ceilings with an elaborate fresco of the sky. The rooms are filled with works of art featuring Gala, including the mystical painting *Gala's Castle at Púbol*, in the Piano Room. Gala was devoted to fashion, and a small collection of her designer clothes are on display. After the comparitive austerity of the interior, the gardens come as a playful surprise. Dalí's elongated sculptures of elephants gambol beneath the hedges, and a fountain by the swimming pool is decorated with the multicoloured heads of the composer Wagner.

THE BASICS

www.salvador-dali.org

✛ G5

✉ Plaça Gala Dalí, Castell de Púbol

☎ 972 48 86 55

🕐 Mid-Jun to mid-Sep daily 10–8; mid-Mar to mid-Jun, mid-Sep to Oct Tue–Sun 10–6; Nov–Dec Tue–Sun 10–5. Closed Jan to mid-Mar

🍽 Can Bosch (€€) in the village

🚌 SARFA bus to La Pera, then 2km (1.2-mile) walk to Púbol, or Flaçà, then 4km (2.5-mile) walk to Púbol

🚆 To Flaçà, then taxi or 30-min walk

♿ Good

✋ Moderate

HIGHLIGHTS

● Paintings of Gala
● Coat-of-Arms Room
● Piano Room
● Gala's bathroom
● Kitchen and gardens

TIP

● For some of the best views in the Costa Brava, visit the Santuari dels Àngels, about 10km (6 miles) from Púbol (follow signs from Madremanya).

Illes Medes

HIGHLIGHTS

- Snorkelling and diving around the islands
- Birdwatching
- Glass-bottomed boat trip

TIP

- There is a strictly controlled maximum of 450 dives a day, so book weeks in advance for a slot during the peak season (mid-July to early September).

The Illes Medes, a rocky archipelago floating just off L'Estartit, is one of the most important nature reserves in the western Mediterranean, and a popular diving and snorkelling destination.

The islands Of the seven islands and islets which make up the archipelago, five are little more than rocky outcrops. The largest, Meda Gran, has been inhabited since the first Greek settlers arrived in the region, and has been a hideout for pirates and a French prison through the centuries. The last inhabitants left in 1934, but a 19th-century lighthouse continues to function nightly. Although the islands are best known for their marine life, they are also a breeding ground for more than 60 species of seabirds (notably the yellow-legged gull,

Clockwise from left: The Illes Medes attract divers, scuba-divers and snorkellers who come to swim among the coral reefs and caves; the islands are a haven for seabirds, including gulls, which breed here between March and May each year; the rocky islets are a continuation of the Montgri Massif

which breeds here in huge numbers), as well as lizards and insects which thrive in the arid conditions.

Flora and fauna The waters around the Illes Medes are extraordinarily rich in flora and fauna, thanks largely to the diversity of depths. Starfish, octopuses and lobsters live in the coral reefs and caves at shallow depths, while the deeper caves and tunnels teem with grouper, conger eels, moray eels, John Dory and scorpion fish. Vast submarine meadows of *Posidonia oceanica* help to keep the waters crystal clear. If diving and snorkelling are not for you, take a trip in a glass-bottomed boat. There are strict regulations limiting the number of visitors to the reserve area: check first with the park authorities in L'Estartit.

THE BASICS

www.parcsdecatalunya.net/medes

🔲 H5

ℹ️ Carrer Eivissa, Edificio Medes Park, L'Estartit, tel 972 75 11 03

🍴 No facilities on the islands, but numerous cafés and restaurants in L'Estartit (€–€€€)

🚌 AMPSA bus from Girona to L'Estartit

♿ Few

Olot

HIGHLIGHTS

● Admiring the landscapes of the School of Olot
● Reliving the 1427 earthquake in the Casal dels Volcans

TIPS

● Olot is famous for its annual festival, the Festes del Tura, in which the *gegants d'Olot* (Giants of Olot) dance through the streets.
● This region is spectacular seen from a hot-air balloon (▷ 60).

Olot came to prominence in the mid-19th century when its soft light and gentle hills inspired a school of landscape painting. The hills are actually volcanoes, long extinct, which provide a glorious green setting for this appealing town.

City centre A handful of Modernista villas are scattered around the centre of Olot, particularly along the Carrer Escultor Miquel Blay. This broad promenade, with its spreading trees and terrace cafés, is named after the most famous Modernista sculptor associated with the town, Miquel Blay. Some of his works, along with early Impressionist-style paintings from the Olot School, are on view at the Museu Comarcal de la Garrotxa (▷ 52). Nearby, a lavish 18th-century mansion, Can Trincheria, is richly

Clockwise from far left: Looking out over the rooftops of Olot, capital of the Garrotxa region; detail on a house in the Rambla; the Modernist Casa Sola Morales; the 19th-century Teatre Principal; the neoclassical parish church of Sant Esteve; view from the Volca de Montsacopa, with the peaks of the Pyrenees in the background

decorated with period furnishings. The Claustre del Carme, a restrained Renaissance cloister which is all that survives of a Carmelite convent, has been incorporated into Olot's art school.

Volcanoes The town's lively old quarter dates from the 15th century: Olot was razed by a massive earthquake in 1427 and had to be entirely rebuilt. The earthquake is recreated in the Casal dels Volcans (▷ 51), which also serves as the information office for the Parc Natural de la Zona Volcànica de la Garrotxa (▷ 53), which surrounds Olot. There are several signposted hiking trails up to the craters of volcanoes from the city. The volcanoes have also been incorporated into local cuisine, which is known as Cuina Volcànica, and focuses on local produce and time-honoured recipes.

THE BASICS

www.turismeolot.cat

✚ C4

🛈 Carrer Hospici 8, tel 972 26 01 41

🍴 Numerous restaurants (€–€€€)

🚌 TEISA bus from Girona

♿ Good

Pals

The village of Pals, abandoned in 1939 after the Civil War, has been lovingly restored

THE BASICS

www.pals.es

🞧 H6

ℹ️ Plaça Major 7, tel 972 63 61 61

🍴 Numerous cafés and restaurants (€–€€€)

🚂 To Flacà, or La Bisbal d'Empordà, then taxi

🚌 Limited SARFA bus service between Pals and Girona

♿ Few

HIGHLIGHTS

● Ca La Pruna cultural centre
● Sunset from the Mirador Josep Pla

TIPS

● Visit nearby Palau-sator, 7km (4 miles) northwest of Pals, which also has a charming Gothic core, but attracts fewer tourists.
● Pals' entire raison d'être is tourism: come out of season and it's a ghost town.

Pals is perhaps the prettiest village in the Empordà. The Gothic town is piled up on a hilltop, with views over the surrounding wetlands, and its winding streets are packed with souvenir shops and taverns.

Medieval village Just a few decades ago Pals was little more than a pile of rubble. It was restored to its original medieval glory after the destruction wrought during the Civil War, and now resembles an immaculate open-air museum, with its narrow passages, perfect squares and fortified towers. The Gothic mansions and town houses have become expensive weekend homes, and restaurants, cafés and craft shops catering for the tourists have opened in the medieval arcades. A good first port-of-call is Ca La Pruna, a 15th-century fortified mansion which now houses the local cultural centre. Cobbled streets wind up to the Plaça Major, where an archway marks the entrance to El Pedró, the original walled citadel. There are wonderful views over the Empordà from the Mirador Josep Pla: come at dusk, if you can, to watch the sunset blaze across the plain.

Beaches Pals also boasts one of the longest beaches on the Costa Brava: 3.5km (2 miles) of golden sands called the Platja de Pals, about 5km (3 miles) from the medieval village. Until 2006, the huge Radio Liberty mast was located on this beach, broadcasting to eastern Europe right up until 2001.

The west door of the Monestir de Santa Maria (left and middle) and the exterior (right)

Ripoll

Ripoll is set amid the pine-clad peaks of the pre-Pyrenees, the traditional heartland of Catalonia. It grew up around a ninth-century monastery, established by Guifré El Pilós (William the Hairy).

The monastery The Monestir de Santa Maria was consecrated in 888, and quickly grew into an important centre of learning, famous for its illuminated manuscripts. It was expanded and rebuilt in the 11th century under abbot Oliba, who ordered the construction of the glorious alabaster portal. This is one of the finest examples of Romanesque art in the world. Scenes from the Bible, the Labours of the Months, saints and fabulous creatures are depicted with astonishing vivacity (it's worth getting the audio guide and explanatory leaflet to identify them all). Inside the church, the bones of William the Hairy are buried in a modern tomb near the altar, but the original sarcophagi of early Catalan counts line the nave. The cloister, another masterpiece of Romanesque art, has survived remarkably intact, its paired columns carved with a medieval menagerie of mythical creatures.

Other sights There's not much else to see in Ripoll, but the Scriptorium, on the Raval de l'Hospital, displays facsimiles of the famous illuminated manuscripts. The Palau Forge, by the river, is a 17th-century foundry, which made nails right up until the 1970s, and is now open for guided tours.

THE BASICS

www.turismeripoll.cat
➕ A4
ℹ️ Plaça de l'Abat Oliba s/n, tel 972 70 23 51
🍴 Numerous cafés and restaurants (€–€€€)
🚆 RENFE train to Ripoll (Barcelona–Puigcerdà line)
🚌 TEISA bus (from Girona)
♿ Few

Monestir de Santa Maria
✉️ Plaça de l'Abat Oliba s/n
🕐 Daily 10–1, 3–6 (until 7pm in winter)

HIGHLIGHTS

● Romanesque portal of Santa Maria
● Scriptorium
● Palau Forge

TIP

● The tourist office offers a range of themed guided tours around the town: families will enjoy 'Ripoll: Five Centuries in the Making'. Tickets (€5, free under-8s).

More to See

BEGUR

www.begur.org

Begur, just inland from the Cap de Begur (▷ 42), has a beguiling old quarter, and is topped by the substantial remains of a castle, which can be climbed for incredible views. The remnants of the medieval walls are studded with towers, and narrow, cobbled streets fan out from the church square. Still very much an upmarket destination, Begur is packed with fancy boutiques, bars and restaurants.
✚ H6 🚹 Avinguda Onze de Setembre 5, tel 972 62 45 20 🍴 Numerous cafés and restaurants (€–€€€) 🚌 SARFA bus from Girona, Barcelona and Palafrugell ♿ Few

LA BISBAL D'EMPORDÀ

www.labisbal.info

La Bisbal is not especially attractive from the outskirts. The medieval centre, although rather worn, is decidedly prettier, particularly during the colourful Friday market. The town was once the seat of the bishops ('bisbal') of Girona, and the crenellated Romanesque episcopal palace still dominates the Plaça del Castell. La Bisbal is famous for its ceramics. It's also considered the traditional home of the *sardana*, the national dance of Catalonia, performed at most local festivals, including the Festa Major (17 Aug).
✚ G6 🚹 Plaça del Castell s/n, tel 972 64 51 66 🍴 Numerous cafés and restaurants (€–€€€) 🚌 SARFA bus from Girona, Barcelona and Palafrugell ♿ Few

CASTELLFOLLIT DE LA ROCA

www.castellfollitdelaroca.org

Tiny Castellfollit de la Roca is strung out spectacularly high on a precipitous cliff of rippling lava. The houses are built of volcanic stone, and the narrow lanes converge at a dramatic *mirador* (lookout point), where you can gaze down at the precipice below. It's famous for its *embutits* (cured sausages), and has a small museum, the Museu d'Embotit (www.museudelembotit. com). The town lies within the Parc Natural de la Zona Volcànica de

View from the ruins of Begur's castle

Castellfollit de la Roca, perched on its basalt promontory

la Garrotxa and is surrounded by hiking trails.

🞣 C4 🛈 Plaça de Sant Roc 2, tel 972 29 40 03 🍴 Limited selection of cafés and restaurants (€–€€) 🚌 TEISA bus from Girona or Olot ♿ Few

L'ESTARTIT

www.visitestartit.com

The former fishing village of L'Estartit has developed into a sizeable tourist resort, with beaches and a large marina backed by apartment blocks. Fishing is no longer the main industry, but a few trawlers still bob about in the harbour. Thanks to the proximity of the Illes Medes (▷ 44–45), L'Estartit is a thriving water-sports destination.

🞣 H5 🛈 Passeig Marítim s/n, tel 972 75 19 10 🍴 Numerous cafés and restaurants (€–€€€) 🚌 SARFA and AMPSA buses from Girona and Barcelona ♿ Good

LLAFRANC

www.visitpalafrugell.cat, www.llafranc.com

Llafranc is curled around an idyllic bay, with plunging cliffs and a perfect crescent of golden sand. It has been a popular resort since the 1950s, and has changed little since then. Development has been kept firmly in check, and the little resort retains its low-key intimacy, even at the height of the season. Coastal paths carved into the rock head south to Calella de Palafrugell (▷ 41) and Tamariu (▷ 54–55), passing secluded bays perfect for picnicking or snorkelling.

🞣 H6 🛈 Carrer Roger de Llúria s/n, tel 972 30 50 08 🍴 Numerous cafés and restaurants (€–€€€) 🚌 SARFA bus from Girona and Barcelona ♿ Few

OLOT: CASAL DELS VOLCANS

www.turismeolot.cat

Olot's Casal dels Volcans occupies a 19th-century villa, the Torre Castanys. The office functions as museum and information office for the Parc Natural de la Zona Volcànica de la Garrotxa (▷ 53). Exhibits describe the history and geology of the region, but the

Olot's Casal dels Volcans in the botanic gardens at Parc Nou

highlight is a short film describing the massive earthquake which shook the region in 1427; the entire audio-visual room shakes ominously, to the delight of kids.

➕ C4 ✉ Avinguda Santa Coloma
☎ 972 62 45 20 🕐 Jul–Sep Tue–Fri 10–2, 4–7, Sat 10–2, 4–7, Sun 11–2; Oct–Jun Tue–Fri 10–2, 3–6, Sat 10–2, 4–7, Sun 11–2
🍴 Small café for drinks and light snacks (€)
🚌 TEISA bus from Girona or Ripoll ♿ Few
👜 Inexpensive

OLOT: MUSEU COMARCAL DE LA GARROTXA

www.turismeolot.cat

Olot's regional museum has an enjoyably diverse collection of artworks, plus an ethnographic section displaying traditional tools. The pre-Impressionistic paintings by the Olot School are impressive, featuring the landscapes which so entranced the 19th-century artists. Perhaps the most famous Olotí is the Modernista sculptor Miquel Blay (1866–1936). Other outstanding Modernista artists represented here include Ramon Casas, an early patron of Picasso, and there's a gorgeous collection of turn-of-the-20th-century posters for a French cigarillo company.

➕ C4 ✉ Avinguda Santa Coloma
☎ 972 26 81 12 🍴 Numerous cafés and restaurants nearby (€–€€€) 🚌 TEISA bus from Girona or Ripoll ♿ Few
👜 Inexpensive

PALAFRUGELL

www.visitpalafrugell.net

Palafrugell preserves vestiges of its original medieval core in La Vil.la, a web of narrow streets near the 11th-century church of Sant Martí. The focal point of the town is the Plaça Nova, where numerous bars and cafés are clustered. Throughout most of the 20th century, the town was an important centre of cork production, and this industry is recalled in the Museu del Suro (www.museudelsuro.cat). An early 20th-century cork factory, Can Mario, now contains a superb collection of contemporary

Les Bugaderes *by Joaquim Vayreda (1883) at the Museu Comarcal de la Garrotxa*

sculpture (www.fundaciovilacasas.com). Palafrugell's port, about 5km (3 miles) away, is now the resort of Calella de Palafrugell (▷ 41).

➕ H6 🛈 Teatre Municipal, Carrer Santa Margarida 1, tel 972 30 02 28 🍽 Numerous cafés and restaurants (€–€€) 🚌 SARFA bus from Girona, Barcelona and along the coast ♿ Few

PARC NATURAL DE LA ZONA VOLCÀNICA DE LA GARROTXA

www.turismegarrotxa.com

The undulating, otherworldy landscape of La Garrotxa is formed by the curious, flattened cones of about 40 long-extinct volcanoes. The region is still considered seismically active, although the last major earthquake, which razed Olot, happened in 1427. Now protected as a nature reserve, the park has numerous excellent hiking trails, some of which visit the strange, marbled craters of the ancient volcanoes. The region is thickly wooded, and contains the most extensive beech forest in Catalonia, the Fageda d'en Jordà, magnificent in autumn.

➕ C4 🛈 Museu Comarcal de la Garrotxa, Avinguda Santa Coloma, Olot, tel 972 26 81 12 🕐 Jul–Sep Tue–Fri 10–2, 4–7, Sat 10–2, 4–7, Sun 11–2; Oct–Jun Tue–Fri 10–2, 3–6, Sat 10–2, 4–7, Sun 11–2 🍽 Small café for drinks and snacks (€) 🚌 TEISA bus from Girona or Ripoll ♿ Few 🎟 Inexpensive

PERATALLADA

www.forallac.com

Peratallada sits on a low hilltop emerging from the flat plain of the Baix Empordà. Cobbled streets lined with immaculately restored stone houses wind up to the remnants of the castle. Vestiges of the medieval walls have survived, as well as the Gothic church of Sant Esteve with its unusual belltower. The town is packed with shops and cafés and there are several fine restaurants in the vicinity.

➕ G5 🛈 Carrer Unió 3, tel 972 64 55 22 🍽 Several cafés and restaurants nearby (€–€€€) 🚌 SARFA bus from Girona and Begur ♿ Few

The belltower of the Church of Sant Esteve in Peratallada

SANT JOAN DE LES ABADESSES

www.santjoandelesabadesses.cat

The town is named for its ninth-century monastery, one of the jewels of Catalan Romanesque architecture. At the entrance to town is the steeply arched Pont Vell, a medieval bridge once used by pilgrims. The Monestir de Sant Joan de les Abadesses has survived impressively intact, and the dim, austere nave is deeply atmospheric. A magnificent 13th-century sculptural group depicting the Descent from the Cross serves as the main altarpiece, and there are more treasures in the museum. A Via Verde cycle path (www.rutadelfierro.net), following an old train line, links Sant Joan de les Abadesses with Ripoll.

🚉 A4 🏛 Palau de l'Abadia, tel 972 72 05 99 🍴 Numerous cafés and restaurants (€–€€€) 🎫 Monastery: Mar–Apr, Oct daily 10–2, 4–6; May–Jun 10–2, 4–7; Jul–Sep 10–7, Sat–Sun 10–2, 4–7; Nov–Feb Mon–Fri 10–2, Sat–Sun 10–2, 4–6 🚌 SARFA bus from Girona, Barcelona and Palafrugell ♿ Few

SANTA PAU

www.santapau.es

Santa Pau is a tiny medieval village encircled by sturdy walls. It lies in the middle of the Parc Natural de la Zona Volcànica de la Garrotxa, and is a perfect base for exploring the area. The miniature 11th-century castle and Plaça Major are a delight, and there's a handful of restaurants, cafés and guest houses, plus a park information centre. Superb walking trails lead out from the town, and balloon rides and horse-riding are on offer.

🚉 C4 🏛 Plaça Major 1, tel 972 68 03 49 🍴 Numerous cafés and restaurants (€–€€€) 🚌 TEISA bus from Olot and Banyoles ♿ Few

TAMARIU

www.visitpalafrugell.cat

The former fishing village of Tamariu has developed into a popular resort, thanks to its sheltered beach and shallow waters, but development is low-key. It has preserved plenty of

View over the Garrotxa Valley from Santa Pau

old-fashioned charm and, although the fishing fleet has long gone, colourful boats still bob in the harbour. The craggy coastline is ideal for snorkelling and diving.

🚑 H6 🛈 Carrer Riera s/n, tel 972 620193 🍴 Numerous cafés and restaurants (€–€€€) 🚌 SARFA or TEISA buses from Girona and Barcelona ♿ Few

TORROELLA DE MONTGRÍ

www.visitestartit.com

The country town of Torroella de Montgrí sits beneath a huge castle-topped crag, visible for miles around. It preserves a small medieval heart, and Plaça de la Vila makes a colourful backdrop for the Monday market. The palace built for the Counts of Torroella de Montgrí between the 9th and 14th centuries is now a luxury hotel. The Museu de la Mediterrània presents fascinating interactive displays on local history and culture. The Montgrí Massif, which stretches behind the town to the coast, is a nature reserve, with superb hiking

trails. A signposted path leads up to the 14th-century castle (1.5 hours), with magnificent views

🚑 H5 🛈 Can Quintana, Carrer Ullà 31, tel 972 75 51 80 🍴 Numerous cafés and restaurants (€–€€€) 🚌 SARFA and AMPSA buses from Girona, Barcelona and the coast ♿ Few

ULLASTRET

www.labisbal.info

The fortified town of Ullastret occupies a hilltop, the Puig de Sant Andreu, just outside the town, and was founded in the sixth century BC. The settlement was encircled by a thick wall, later extended and heavily fortified, which has survived astonishingly intact. A small museum gives the historical context for the ruins, with displays of finds and audio-visuals.

🚑 G5 🛈 Afores s/n, Puig de Sant Andreu, tel 972 17 90 58 🕐 Jun–Sep Tue–Sun 10–8; Oct–May Tue–Sun 10–2, 3–6; Easter weekend 10–8 🍴 A few cafés and restaurants (€–€€) 🚊 To Flacà, then taxi 🚌 SARFA bus from Girona and the coast to Ullastret ♿ Few

The sparkling turquoise waters of Tamariu bay

Remains of the Iberian settlement at Ullastret, the largest yet discovered in Catalonia

A Walk to Castell de Montgrí

The Montgrí Massif offers spellbinding views over the entire Gulf of Roses and back to the Pyrenees.

DISTANCE: 10km (6 miles)   **ALLOW:** 3 hours

START

TORROELLA DE MONTGRÍ
H5   SARFA or TEISA bus

1 Start in Passeig de Catalunya, in the centre of town. Follow signs for 'Castell de Montgrí – Zona Esportiva', to reach a car park next to a school.

2 A paved path leads through olive trees and pine groves and, just after a house called 'El Xaloc', the tarmac runs out and the dirt path begins to narrow. Red-and-white markings denote the GR92 (a long-distance walking path).

3 Follow the narrow path upwards for about 45 minutes to the castle at the summit, which has views over a great swathe of central Catalonia.

4 There's a flat area near the castle marked with several trails. Follow the red-and-white signs for the GR92 to the Cim de Montplà (Montplà summit) with more views.

END

TORROELLA DE MONTGRÍ

7 This local path culminates in the GI-641, the busy main road between Torroella and L'Estartit. You will have to walk on the side of the road to reach the unpaved walking trail, which runs parallel to the road. It's about 800m (875 yards) back into town.

6 Shortly after the picnic area, leave the GR92 and turn right, following the green-and-white signs indicating a local path. This leads through a residential development to a road, the Camí de les Dunes, in about 25 minutes. Turn right onto another local path (with green-and-white markings).

5 The path begins to descend, with more incredible vantage points. After about 45 minutes, you'll reach Les Dunes, a beautiful protected area formed by drifting sand, with wooden tables for picnicking.

A Drive from Banyoles

This drive takes you into the cradle of Catalonia, the former haunt of legendary leader Wilfred the Hairy.

DISTANCE: 128km (80 miles)   **ALLOW:** 9–12 hours, including visits

START

BANYOLES
🚌 E4 🚌 TEISA bus from Girona

❶ From Banyoles, take the GI524 towards Santa Pau (24km/15 miles west), heading into the volcanic, forest-covered hills of La Garrotxa (▷ 53).

❷ Turn left into the village of Santa Pau (▷ 54), a walled medieval village crowned with a castle. Return to the GI524 and continue to Olot, a further 10km (6 miles) west.

❸ Wander through the lively old centre of Olot (▷ 46–47). There are plenty of options here for lunch

❹ Follow the scenic N-260 (rather than the faster C-26) to Ripoll (▷ 49), 36km (22 miles) west of Olot, to admire the spectacular Romanesque portal of the Monestir de Santa Maria.

END

BANYOLES

❽ From Besalú, it's another 14km (8.5 miles) along the C-66 to return to the lakeside resort of Banyoles (▷ 38–39).

❼ The A26 whisks you in moments to the medieval village of Besalú (▷ 40).

❻ Take the fast C-26 for 26km (16 miles) west to Castellfollit de la Roca (▷ 50–51), perched high on its lava-striped cliff. Stroll around the village and pick up some *embutits* (cured sausages), a local speciality.

❺ From Ripoll, it's a short drive north along the N-260 to Sant Joan de les Abadesses (11km/7 miles). The entrancing and austere monastery of Sant Joan de les Abadesses dominates the little town, and is another jewel of Catalan Romanesque art (▷ 54).

Shopping

AGROBOTIGA

This little shop in the middle of Santa Pau's atmospheric old quarter sells the region's most famous gourmet product: *fesols de Santa Pau*. These tasty white beans are the traditional accompaniment to *butifarra*, Catalan sausages, and the beans from the Santa Pau region are deemed the finest in Spain.

➕ C4 ✉ Carrer Major 14, Santa Pau ☎ 972 68 00 78

ANTICS BISBAL

La Bisbal has long been famous for its pottery, but it's also home to a number of excellent antiques shops, and even hosts a prestigious biannual antiques fair. This appealingly cluttered store has a huge range of objects, dating from medieval times to the turn-of-the-20th century.

➕ G6 ✉ Carrer Sis d'Octubre 79, La Bisbal d'Empordà ☎ 972 64 34 83

BAMBU BAMBU

www.bambubambu.com
Bambu Bambu is packed with wicker garden furniture, as well as a range of textiles and decorative objects for the home. It stands out among the countless ceramic shops which line Carrer Aigüeta on the outskirts of La Bisbal.

➕ G6 ✉ Carrer Aigüeta 61, La Bisbal d'Empordà ☎ 972 64 23 33

CA LA MARIONA

This is dedicated to gourmet goodies from around Spain, with an excellent choice of local wines, cheeses, oils, hams, charcuterie, chocolate, preserves and more. Great for gifts, or for a really special picnic.

➕ C4 ✉ Carrer Sant Rafel 23, Olot ☎ 972 26 38 70

CAN GRAU

A tiny workshop in the heart of Besalú, Can Grau is run by Joan Grau Cànoves, who sells his own delightful artworks—delicate paintings and beautiful stained glass (lights, decorative objects, mirrors, picture frames and more).

➕ D4 ✉ Plaça del Prat de Sant Pere 14, Besalú ☎ 972 59 12 85

MARKETS

The weekly market is still very much part of village life throughout Catalonia. Here you'll find all kinds of wonderful fresh produce, from incredible heaps of fruit and vegetables, to handmade cheeses and cured meats. During the summer, many resorts host evening craft markets along the seafront, and, in recent years, medieval markets, which might include displays of folk dancing as well as stalls selling tradi-tional foodstuffs and crafts, have become very popular with both locals and tourists.

CARNISSERIA PUJOLAR

Castellfollit de la Roca is well known throughout Catalonia for its delicious cured sausages *(embutits)*. This shop raises its own pigs and prepares the meat according to time-honoured traditions.

➕ C4 ✉ Carretera de Girona 2, Castellfollit de la Roca ☎ 972 29 45 21

CASA ORDIALES

This long-established family-run business has a wide range of jewellery, from exquisite pieces with precious stones, to elegant costume jewellery. It also sells watches and gift items.

➕ G6 ✉ Carrer Riera 4, La Bisbal d'Empordà ☎ 972 64 52 48

CONCEP GUAL JOIE

www.concepgual.com
This sleek, vaulted boutique displays a wide range of original, contemporary jewellery, necklaces, bracelets and rings. Look for the beautiful long necklaces with jewelled 'talismans' inspired by the exquisite coves of the nearby Cap de Begur.

➕ H6 ✉ Camí del Mar 4, Begur ☎ 972 19 05 81

FANG I ART

The Carrer de l'Aigüeta, on the edge of La Bisbal, is lined with pottery shops. This one promises that all its wares are

made by hand in their own workshops. Pick up terracotta water jars, which keep water cool all day, and some colourfully painted plant pots.

🏠 G6 ✉ Carrer de l'Aigüeta 76, La Bisbal d'Empordà ☎ 972 64 39

LLIBRERIA EL DRAC

This charming bookshop occupies the ground floor of one of the finest Modernista mansions in Olot, the Casa Gaieta. Browse among its superb selection of books, which are mostly but not exclusively in Catalan, and include some beautiful photography books, maps and walking guides.

🏠 C4 ✉ Passeig d'en Blai 61, Olot ☎ 972 26 10 30

MANOLITA

This old-fashioned spot in the heart of Palafrugell serves all kinds of delicious olives. Try the spicy ones with a touch of chilli, or the plump green manzanilla olives stuffed with anchovies. You will also find *bacallà*, salted cod, which has been popular around the Mediterranean for centuries, but is rather an acquired taste.

🏠 H6 ✉ Plaça del Mercat, Palafrugell ☎ 972 30 15 83

PASTISSERIA I BOMBONERIA CAN CARBÓ

Stop at this bakery on the main square in Banyoles to collect the essentials for a lakeside picnic—wonderfully fresh bread, delicious pastries and cakes, and divine chocolates, all beautifully packaged.

🏠 E4 ✉ Plaça Major, 19, Banyoles ☎ 972 57 04 28

PASTISSERIA SANS

The delightful family-owned Pastisseria Sans, opened in 1927, is still going strong, and is now run by the third generation of the family. It is famous locally for the scrumptious *bisbalenc*, a pastry stuffed with *cabell de l'àngel* ('angel hair', a kind of pumpkin jam) or marzipan. It also sells freshly made Catalan savoury dishes to take away.

🏠 G6 ✉ Avinguda Voltes 4, La Bisbal d'Empordà ☎ 972 64 03 75

RULDUÀ CERÀMICA

www.rulduaceramica.com
La Bisbal is crammed with ceramic shops, part of a tradition in the region which dates back to the Middle Ages. This little shop is conveniently located in the centre of town, and has a wide range of gift items, including delightful handpainted tiles. The spotty kitchenware is also very pretty.

🏠 G6 ✉ Plaça de la Llibertat, La Bisbal d'Empordà ☎ 972 64 10 17

TERRA I FOC

One of several small gift shops within the walled village of Pals, Terra I Foc sells brightly coloured pottery, postcards and T-shirts.

🏠 H6 ✉ Carrer Muralla 4, Pals ☎ 972 63 71 18

VINS I LICORS GRAU

www.vinsilicorsgrau.es
This huge warehouse has an enormous array of wines, liqueurs and spirits, all at reasonable prices. There's an award-winning range of wines, with more than 800 labels, including a well-chosen selection from the Empordà. There is a small tasting area, where you can have a bottle of wine opened for a small corkage fee, and try some simple tapas. They also offer a delivery service.

🏠 H6 ✉ Carrer Torroella 163, Palafrugell ☎ 972 30 18 35

Entertainment and Activities

BAR ES CASTELL

A relaxed, old-fashioned bar on the main square, this is good for an early evening glass of wine and some tapas as you watch the crowds ebb and flow. It's one of several good options on the square.
➕ H6 ✉ Plaça de la Vila 4, Begur ☎ 972 62 20 04 🕐 Daily 12–12

BEGUR DIVE

www.begurdive.com
Begur Dive offers a wide range of dives around the magnficent Cap de Begur, as well as diving courses and equipment hire.
➕ H6 ✉ Carretera d'Esclanyà km 2, Platja d'Aiguablava, Begur ☎ 609 437 106

CENTRE D'ESQUÍ I ACTIVITATS AQUÀTIQUES SKI-BUS

www.ski-bus.es
This school will teach you to waterski (courses for children and adults) on this popular beach on the Cap de Begur. It also rents out banana boats, rings and wakeboards.
➕ H6 ✉ Platja del Racó, Begur ☎ 657 851 570

LA DEVESA DE TOR

www.ladevesadetor.com
A 400-year-old stone *masía* in the countryside has been converted into an enchanting and very unusual bar—La Devesa de Tor. The quirky decoration combines leopard-skin sofas with glittering chandeliers, and the huge garden is magically lit with candles. Come for drinks, light snacks and regular live music.
➕ G4 ✉ Carrer del Mar 3, Tor ☎ 972 78 06 23 🕐 Jun–Sep Mon–Sat 10pm–3am, Sun 7pm–3am; Oct–May Wed–Sat 10pm–3am, Sun 7pm–3am

ESCOLA NÀUTICA DE PALS

www.capgirell.net
The beach at Pals is a magnet for windsurfers and kitesurfers. This sailing school offers equipment for rent

GOLF

There are several outstanding golf courses on the Costa Brava, including:
Golf Plata de Pals, Camí del Golf, tel 972 66 77 39, www.golfplatjadepals.com;
Golf Costa Brava, Santa Cristina d'Aro, tel 927 83 71 50, www.golfcostabrava.com;
Club Golf d'Aro, Urb Mas Nou, Platja d'Aro, tel 972 82 69 00, www.golfdaro.com;
Empordà Golf, Carretera de Torroella a Palafrugell s/n, Gualta, tel 972 76 04 50, www.empordagolf.com;
Golf Serres de Pals, Pals, tel 972 63 73 75, www.golfserresdepals.com;
PGA Golf de Catalunya, Ctra N-II, km 701, Caldes de Malavella, tel 972 47 25 77, www.pgacatalunya.com.

and for sale, as well as lessons in windsurfing, kayaking, kitesurfing and sailing.
➕ H5 ✉ Carrer Enginyer Algarra 10, Platja de Pals ☎ 629 881 216

LUX CAFÉ

www.luxolot.com
Lux Café is a fashionable lounge-style hangout in Olot featuring local DJs, live music and regular theme parties. Check the website for events.
➕ C4 ✉ Carrer Marià Jollis Pellicer 36, Olot ☎ 972 27 23 89 🕐 Sep–Jul Thu–Sun 10pm–3am

NOCTÀMBUL

A relaxed and friendly music bar in the heart of old Begur, where you can order a mojito, the house speciality, and relax over a game of table football or darts. Football and other big sports events are shown on a giant screen.
➕ H6 ✉ Carrer Pi i Rallo 23, Begur ☎ 654 353 905 🕐 Daily 8pm–late

VOL DE COLOMS

www.voldecoloms.cat
Numerous companies offer balloon rides over the Garrotxa region. This company is based in Santa Pau, and offers a wonderful early morning flight, complete with cava and *coca dels llardons* (a traditional pastry), followed by a country breakfast in Santa Pau.
➕ C4 ✉ Santa Pau ☎ 972 68 02 55

Restaurants

PRICES

Prices are approximate, based on a 3-course meal for one person.

€€€	over €45
€€	€25–€45
€	under €25

CAN BONAY (€€)

www.bonay.com

Can Bonay prides itself on using time-honoured Catalan recipes, and you'll find delicious stews, grills and casseroles along with fresh fish from the coast. There's a 'wine museum' in the basement, with a wine store next door. Summer terrace.

➕ G5 ✉ Plaça de les Voltes 13, Peratallada ☎ 972 63 40 34 🕐 Lunch and dinner; closed Mon, except public hols

CAN ROCA (€€)

A traditional inn in a tiny village about 8km (5 miles) east of Besalú, this is a great place to try typical Catalan favourites such as *canelones* (canelloni stuffed with meat or vegetables), *butifarra amb mongetes* (pork sausages with beans) and rich game dishes in winter.

➕ E4 ✉ Avinguda Carles Fortuny 1, Esponellà ☎ 972 59 70 12 🕐 Lunch and dinner; closed dinner Mon–Fri in winter

CASA RUDES (€)

Casa Rudes serves tasty Catalan country cooking. Try the venison and wild mushrooms in season, or go for classics like *butifarra amb mongetes* (pork sausage and beans). The adjoining shop sells *embutits* (cured sausages) and other local produce.

➕ A4 ✉ Carrer Major 10, Sant Joan de les Abadesses ☎ 972 72 05 07 🕐 Lunch and dinner; closed Sun dinner

LA CASONA (€€)

Traditional Catalan cuisine with modern touches is offered at this rustic inn, where locals recommend the *peus de porc* (pigs' trotters) with lobster, or the *suquet del peix* (fish stew). In spring, you can try the highly prized local delicacy, *garoinada* or *eriçons del mar* – sea anemones.

➕ H6 ✉ Paratge la Sauleda 4, Palafrugell

GAROINADA

Every year in early spring (Jan–Mar), Catalans gather in the Baix Empordà for the *Garoinada*, a feast prepared with sea anemones (*eriçons de mar*, *garotes* or *garoines* in Catalan). Although they are found elsewhere in Spain, the flesh of the Catalan variety is said to be especially sweet. Restaurants in the region, particularly in Palafrugell, Calella de Palafrugell, Llafranc and Tamariu, offer special set menus showcasing the spiky sea creatures.

☎ 972 30 36 61 🕐 Lunch and dinner; closed Sun dinner, Mon and Nov to mid-Dec.

LA CISTERNA (€€)

This is a local favourite, serving great food at reasonable prices. It has a range of set-price menus, featuring sophisticated dishes such as millefeuille with apple, foie gras and goat's cheese, or lamb stuffed with dates.

➕ E4 ✉ Carrer Paissos Catalans 36, Banyoles ☎ 972 58 13 56 🕐 Lunch and dinner; closed Mon

LA CROISSANTERIA DE LLAFRANC (€)

This popular café is good for everything from fresh juice and a pastry in the morning, to a lunchtime coffee and sandwich, or even a chilled beer on the terrace in the evening.

➕ H6 ✉ Plaça Promontori 5, Llafranc ☎ 972 30 51 52 🕐 Daily lunch and dinner

LA DEU (€€–€€€)

www.ladeu.es

Classic Catalan cuisine is on the menu here, with succulent dishes such as stuffed shoulder of lamb and *sarsuela* (Catalan bouillabaisse), but the house speciality is *patates de la deu* – local potatoes, meat and vegetables with béchamel sauce.

➕ C4 ✉ Carretera La Deu s/n, Olot ☎ 972 261 10 04 🕐 Lunch and dinner; closed Sun lunch

DOTZE (€)

The arty Dotze café-bar, in Begur's old quarter, has a delightful little terrace with multicoloured throws and lanterns. Come for superb grilled meats, home-made burgers, hummus and original salads.

🔢 H6 ⊠ Carrer Concepció Pi Tató 12, Begur ☎ 972 62 35 85 ⏰ Daily lunch and dinner

FONDA CANER (€€)

http://fondacaner.com
Fonda Caner is a good place to try the local speciality *peix de roca* (rockfish), or the Catalan version of paella—*rossejat de fideus*—prepared with tiny noodles instead of rice.

🔢 H6 ⊠ Carrer Pi i Ralló 19, Begur ☎ 972 62 30 15 ⏰ Lunch and dinner; closed Sun dinner, Mon

HOSTAL RESTAURANT PUIG SA LLANÇA (€)

This country inn, which also has simple rooms, offers tasty home cooking in a stone-vaulted dining room. It's very popular weekday lunchtimes for the bargain lunch menu (under €10).

🔢 D4 ⊠ Pujada Sant Pere 5, Mieres ☎ 972 68 01 89 ⏰ Lunch and dinner; closed Sun dinner and Mon

LA MAGRANA (€€)

La Magrana is an intimate little café-restaurant which serves traditional Catalan fare like *faves a la Catalana* (broad beans cooked with cured sausage and bacon). It also has a few vegetarian dishes (the mushroom tart is delicious), as well as stir-fries.

🔢 E4 ⊠ Plaça Major 10, Banyoles ☎ 972 57 25 49 ⏰ Lunch and dinner; closed Sun, Mon and public hols

MAS POU (€€)

www.maspou.com
Thick stone walls and beamed ceilings give this classic restaurant plenty of old-fashioned charm. Try the succulent duck with pears. Reservations are essential in summer, particularly if you want a table on the terrace.

🔢 G5 ⊠ Plaça de la Mota 4, Palau-sator ☎ 972 63 41 25 ⏰ Lunch and dinner; closed dinner Sun (except in Aug), Mon and Jan

---

MENÚ DEL DÍA

After the devastation of the Civil War, General Franco established the custom of the *menú del día* (menu of the day) to ensure the workers received a nutritious, inexpensive meal. The tradition has endured and most restaurants offer a two- or three-course meal, usually with wine and bread, Monday to Friday, with an average price of around €8 to €12. Many of the very smartest places offer a fixed-price lunch menu, and it rarely tops €25.

RESTAURANTE EL FAR (€€–€€€)

The El Far restaurant offers superb seafood, served out on a terrace with peerless views of the glorious coastline. It's pricy, but has a *menú del día* (around €20).

🔢 H6 ⊠ Platja de Llafranc s/n, Llafranc ☎ 972 30 16 39 ⏰ Lunch and dinner; closed early Jan–early Feb

RESTAURANT XADÓ (€)

www.restaurantxado.com
The menu offers Mediterranean fare and Moroccan specialities, so you could go for the *arròs Xadó* (a version of paella) or the lamb couscous. Finish with a home-made dessert like a fig pastry with nuts. The set lunch menu is a very reasonable €12.

🔢 H6 ⊠ Carrer Corts Catalanes 12, Palafrugell ☎ 972 30 44 28 ⏰ Lunch and dinner; closed Sun dinner, Mon, Tue in winter

SOL BLANC (€€)

A handsome, ivy-covered country house makes a fine backdrop for the elegant Catalan cuisine here. Prime local produce is key (including vegetables from their own garden), and the dishes are accompanied by a fine selection of Empordan wines.

🔢 H6 ⊠ Carrer Veïnat Molinet 14, Pals ☎ 972 66 73 65 ⏰ Lunch and dinner; closed Tue and Nov

The North Coast and Beyond

The Costa Brava is at its wildest to the north, particularly around the remote Cap de Creus, with its fishing villages and secret coves.

0   5 km
0   3 miles

Cala de Portbou
Portbou
Punta del Claper

Punta dels Canons
Platja de Garbet
Colera   Cap Ras
Grifeu   Cala de Canyelles
          Illa del Castellar
      Llançà
Setcases   Cap Gros
      la Vall de   el
      St Creu   Golfet   Punta dels Farallons
Serra   de   **el Port de**   Illa de Portaló
          Rodes   **la Selva**   Cala de Culip
                  la Selva   Illa s'Encalladora
Monestir de   de Mar   Illa de Massa d'Oros
Sant Pere de   **Portlligat**   **Cap de Creus**
Rodes   ▲   Punta Codera
Palau-   670   Illa de Portlligat
averdera   Rodes
Mas Fumats ■   **Cadaqués**
                                    Punta de s' Oliguera
la Garriga ■   613   s'Arenella
                    ▲   Badia de Cadaqués
                  el Pení
      Roses
Santa
Margarida ■   Mas Oliva   Punta de sa Figuera
      Badia   Canyelles ■   Cala Joncols
      de Roses   Almadrava ■   Cap de Norfeu
Empuriabrava   Cap Trencat
                  Punta Falconera
Platja de
Empuriabrava

Golf de Roses

St Martí d'Empúries
Empúries
      l'Escala
es Corts ■   Punta de la Clota Grossa
      Riells   Punta de Trecabranços
            Cala Montgó

Badia de Port de la Selva

H   **J**

Cadaqués

Views of Cadaqués (left and right); statue of Salvador Dalí on the seafront (middle)

THE BASICS

www.visitcadaques.org
🔶 H3
ℹ️ Carrer Cotxe 1, tel 972 25 83 15
🚌 SARFA bus from Figueres and Roses
♿ Few

HIGHLIGHTS

● The 16th-century parish church
● Museu de Cadaqués
● The GR92 walking path
● Swimming and snorkelling

TIP

● Many of the old streets (including Carrer d'en Call) are still traditionally cobbled in an unusual herringbone pattern, which helps the water run downhill. Carrer de la Sirena is named after a voluptuous mermaid (*sirena* in Catalan) created in the cobblestones.

Cadaqués is a magical, whitewashed village at the tip of the Cap de Creus. The natural beauty and extraordinary light have long attracted artists, including Picasso and Salvador Dalí.

Artistic associations Until little more than a century ago, the village was virtually cut off from the rest of the region by the mountains. Wine and fishing were the main industries, until phylloxera killed the vines in the early 1800s and forced hundreds to emigrate to the Americas. Cadaqués owes its change in fortune to Salvador Dalí, the Surrealist artist, who summered here in the early 20th century and pronounced himself enamoured of the 'divine' light. His artist friends soon followed, and then Dalí sealed his association with the village by building a home in nearby Portlligat (▷ 76).

Beaches and walks The little town is piled up around a simple church, and hugs a glorious bay. There is just a small sandy beach here, but the pristine coastline is studded with pebbly coves, most of which are accessible only by boat or via the panoramic coastal path (GR92, ▷ 119). Cadaqués is now a chic little resort, and smart galleries and boutiques line the narrow streets. The Museu de Cadaqués (open summer only) hosts temporary exhibitions with a Dalí theme. Even though the town can get uncomfortably crowded in the peak summer season, it preserves a dreamy, otherworldliness during the rest of the year.

Cap de Creus

The lighthouse and restaurant (left) have panoramic views over Cap de Creus (right)

The Cap de Creus, the last lunge of the Pyrenees before they drop into the Mediterranean, is a wild, wind-whipped headland, and now a protected nature reserve.

Hikes and views The park information office for the nature reserve is in the monastery of Sant Pere de Rodes (▷ 72–73), which sits above El Port de la Selva (▷ 81). The office has leaflets detailing the network of walking paths signposted throughout the reserve, including the sections of the long distance GR trails (GR11 and GR92) which cross the headland. The monastery is also a good starting point for some excellent hikes, including a stiff climb up to the ruins of the medieval Castell de Sant Salvador.

Flora and fauna The park preserves an extraordinary variety of flora and fauna, and is well known for the rare bird species it protects. It is even better known for its submarine plant and animal life, and the coastline is a magnet for divers and snorkellers. Many of the breathtaking coves are accessible only by boat: these can be rented in Cadaqués (▷ 66).

Lighthouse The Cap de Creus is the easternmost point of mainland Spain. Out at the very tip of the headland is a whitewashed lighthouse, El Far Cap de Creus, with a *mirador* (lookout point) which has panoramic views in all directions.

THE BASICS

www.parcsdecatalunya.net
www. gencat.cat/parcs/
cap_de_creus/
⊞ J2
ℹ Park information office, Palau de l'Abat, Monestir de Sant Pere de Rodes, El Port de la Selva, tel 972 19 31 91
🚌 SARFA bus from Figueres and Roses
♿ Few

HIGHLIGHTS

● Cadaqués, Portlligat, Monestir de Sant Pere de Rodes—all within the park boundaries
● Hiking paths
● Snorkelling and diving around the protected coast
● The views from El Far (the lighthouse)

TIP

● There's a restaurant at the lighthouse, with a terrace to enjoy the incredible views, and an information office.

Empúries

HIGHLIGHTS

● Roman mosaic in the Roman villa
● Site museum
● Seafront promenade (Passeig Marítim)

TIP

● There is a wonderful coastal path, the Passeig Marítim, which links the ruins of Empúries with L'Escala, 1km (0.5 miles) to the south, and Sant Martí d'Empúries, 1km (0.5 miles) to the north. It is only open in summer.

The ancient settlement of Empúries sits serenely amid pine forest overlooking a golden bay. The oldest Greco-Roman settlement in Spain, it was from here that the Romans began their conquest of the entire Iberian peninsula.

History From the seventh century BC, Phoenicians, Etruscans and Greeks came to trade with local tribes who occupied a number of villages in the region. Greeks from Massalia (modern Marseilles) made a permanent settlement here around 580BC, which rapidly grew. When the Romans arrived in 218BC, Emporiae had its own currency and trade links across the Mediterranean. A new, larger Roman city was built directly behind the original settlement, with splendid mansions, an amphitheatre and a

Clockwise from far left: Well-preserved mosaic in one of the Roman villas; a statue of Asclepius, the Greek god of healing (the original is in Barcelona's archaeological museum); looking out over part of the Greek city ruins; the original Greek jetty on the seafront; more of the old Greek city

grand forum. Within two centuries, the Romans controlled the entire peninsula. During the third century AD, Empúries was eclipsed by Barcino (Barcelona) and Tarracó (Tarragona) down the coast and, with the collapse of the Roman Empire, it declined further. Sacked by the Normans in the ninth century, and razed by the North Africans in 935, it was finally abandoned.

Highlights Excavation of the site began in 1909, and less than 25 per cent of the ruins have been explored. A splendid black-and-white mosaic, which adorned the finest Roman villa, has survived, but the most famous discovery is a statue of Asclepius, the god of medicine, one of the finest classical artworks in all of Spain. It has been magnificently restored and enjoys pride of place in the excellent little museum.

THE BASICS

✚ G4

ℹ Carrer Puig i Cadafalch s/n, Empúries-L'Escala, tel 972 77 02 08

🕐 Jun–Sep daily 10–8; Oct–May daily 10–6

🚌 SARFA bus from L'Escala, Girona or Barcelona

♿ Good

✋ Inexpensive

❓ Guided visits by costumed attendants Sun at 12

Figueres: Teatre-Museu Dalí

Salvador Dalí transformed the ruins of the local theatre in Figueres into the world's largest surreal object, topped by a gigantic geodesic dome. Crammed with surreal artworks, it is now one of Spain's top tourist attractions.

The building Dalí was born in Figueres in 1904, and remained very attached to the city throughout his life. In the 1960s, he chose the ruins of the municipal theatre as the site for a new museum dedicated to his works, explaining that it was the perfect setting for an 'eminently theatrical' artist. The building's huge glassy dome and surreal egg-shaped protuberances appear to float above the rooftops. Dalí designed every detail, and endowed the museum with a number of

Weird and wonderful shapes at the Teatre-Museu Dalí, one of the most visited museums in Spain, include Dalí's trademark eggs on the roof and facade and the unmissable transparent geodesic dome

artworks from his private collection, as well as creating several pieces for it. The result is the world's largest array of Dalí artworks.

Museum highlights Among the most striking pieces in the museum is *Cadillac Plujós (The Rainy Cadillac)*, which occupies the central patio: the rain falls inside the 1940s Cadillac, while a statue of a plump diva stands on the bonnet. Another gallery, the Sala Mae West (Mae West Room), seems innocuous at first, but, viewed from atop a ladder supported by a camel, it becomes apparent that the sofa and curtains morph into the features of the legendary actress. Since 2001, the artworks have been adjoined by a spectacular jewellery collection, Dalí-Joies, with more than 30 bejewelled pieces designed by the artist.

THE BASICS

✚ F3

✉ Plaça Gala-Salvador Dalí 5

☎ 972 67 75 00

🕐 Mar–May, Oct Tue–Sun 9.30–6; Jun daily 9.30–6; Jul–Sep daily 9–8; Nov–Feb Tue–Sun 10.30–6

🍴 Numerous cafés and restaurants nearby (€–€€€)

🚌 SARFA and TEISA buses from Girona and other destinations

♿ Few

💲 Expensive

Monestir de Sant Pere de Rodes

TOP **25**

HIGHLIGHTS

- Main church
- Cloister
- Belltower
- Fragments of murals by the atrium

TIPS

- Come in the morning if possible: it can be gloomy in the afternoon when the sun shifts off the mountain.
- There are outstanding views over the Cap de Creus from the upper storey of the cloister.

The huge Romanesque monastery of Sant Pere de Rodes sits high on a mountain overlooking the fishing village of El Port de la Selva. Now a peaceful and isolated spot, it was once one of Spain's most important pilgrimage destinations.

Legends and history The monastery's roots are still shrouded in legend. Some believe that the site was first occupied by a Roman temple dedicated to Venus, goddess of love; this was later converted into a Christian church which gave refuge to three monks escaping Rome, under siege, in the seventh century. They brought with them some of the Catholic church's holiest relics—the head and right arm of St. Peter (Sant Pere in Catalan). By the 11th century, it was surpassed only by Santiago

Clockwise from far left: The belltower and defence tower of the monastery of Sant Pere de Rodes; the winding road from the ruined castle of Sant Salvador; approaching the monastery from the chapel of Santa Helena; view towards the coast from the path behind the monastery; looking up inside the belltower

de Compostela as a place of pilgrimage. The monastery was grandly rebuilt in Romanesque style, when an exquisitely sculpted portal and cloister were added in the 12th century. From the 14th century, wars, plagues and the Black Death put an end to the monastery's Golden Age. The monks finally abandoned it in the early 19th century, and its unique artworks were plundered by collectors.

Cloister and belltower After extensive renovations, the monastery is open to the public. Although much of the complex had to be reconstructed, most of the church, what remains of the cloister and the belltower are original. The setting is breathtaking, with views over the Gulf of Roses. Several superb hiking trails strike out from the monastery grounds.

THE BASICS

➕ H2

✉ Camí del Monestir s/n, El Port de la Selva

☎ 972 19 40 04

🕐 Jun–Sep Tue–Sun 10–7.30; Oct–May Tue–Sun 10–5

🍽 Café-restaurant (€€), open same hours as monastery, also evenings Jul and Aug by reservation

🚌 SARFA bus from Girona and Cadaqués

♿ Few

👋 Moderate

Parc Natural de l'Aigua-molls de l'Empordà

TOP 25

HIGHLIGHTS

● Admiring the spectacular birdlife
● Picnic on the beach

TIPS

● Wear long cotton clothes and douse yourself liberally with mosquito repellent: the insects can be very annoying.
● The birds are best spotted early morning and at dusk.
● The best bases for exploring the park are the towns of Castelló d'Empúries and Sant Pere Pescador.

These extensive wetlands preserve one of the only stretches of virgin coastline on the Costa Brava, and are home to a wide variety of plant and animal life. The park is now the second most important refuge for wetland birds in Spain.

Diverse habitats The nature reserve occupies a vast swathe of coastline between the rivers Muga and Fluvià. It protects diverse habitats which include fresh- and saltwater marshes and lagoons, salt flats, riverine forest and the enclosed, flooded meadows called *closes,* which are unique to this region.

Flora and fauna More than 320 species of bird have been spotted within the park, of which around 90—including stone-curlews,

Dunes, saltflats and wetlands make up a major part of this nature park, where you can find good walks and waymarked trails, abundant birdlife and a vast array of plants and animals, which have made this peaceful refuge, well away from the crowded beaches, their home

black-winged stilts and marsh harriers—breed here. It's also Spain's only nesting ground for the garganey, a rare kind of duck, and is home to one of only two Spanish colonies of the lesser grey shrike. The purple gallinule and white stork were successfully reintroduced here, and have now spread to other wetlands in Catalonia. During the migration periods (Feb–Jun, Jul–Oct), resident numbers are swelled with exotic migrants like spoonbills, glossy ibises, red-crested pochard, short-eared owls and common cranes, as well as many other species. Among the mammals here are the elusive otter, the polecat and fallow deer.

Trails The information centre at El Cortalet provides maps and leaflets, and is the starting point for a pair of great trails around the park.

THE BASICS

➕ G3

ℹ️ Park information office: El Cortalet, Carretera de Sant Pere Pescador km 13.6, Castelló d'Empúries, tel 972 45 42 22

🕐 Apr–Sep daily 9.30–2, 4.30–7; Oct–Mar daily 9.30–2, 3.30–6

🍴 No café on site, but restaurants and cafés in Sant Pere Pescador (€–€€€)

🚌 To Castelló d'Empúries or Sant Pere Pescador

♿ Few. One park trail has been specially adapted for wheelchair users

🎟️ Free

Portlligat: Casa-Museu Salvador Dalí

The Casa-Museu (left and middle) offers good views of the coast (right)

THE BASICS

✚ H2
✉ Portlligat
☎ 972 25 10 15
🕐 9 Feb–14 Jun,
16 Sep–6 Jan Tue–Sun
10.30–6; 15 Jun–15 Sep
daily 9.30–9
🍽 Café-restaurant (€€)
🚌 SARFA bus from
Figueres, Roses and other
places
♿ Few
💶 Expensive
❓ Book admission tickets
at least two days in advance

HIGHLIGHTS

● Polar bear lobby
● Dalí's bedroom
● Gala's whispering chamber
● Patio and swimming pool
● Views of Portlligat harbour

TIP

● Visitors are admitted in
carefully timed groups of 8;
book tickets well in advance,
and pick them up at least 30
minutes before your visit.

Dalí built his home in a whitewashed fisherman's cottage overlooking a perfect, islet-flecked bay. Although he included some Surrealist touches, his home is surprisingly simple and intimate.

History and people Dalí acquired the house in 1930, and lived here with his wife and muse, Gala. It was gradually extended over the following 40 years, a slow accretion of rooms and chambers which were crammed with paintings and personal mementoes. The pair lived here right up until Gala's death in 1982. Dalí produced many of his most famous works in Portlligat, and the beautiful bay figures prominently in scores of his paintings.

Interior and patio At the entrance to the house, a huge stuffed polar bear draped in jewellery greets visitors. From here, corridors, stairways and rooms unfold organically. Among the highlights are Dalí's bedroom, where an ingenious system of mirrors ensures that the rising sun is reflected directly onto the artist's canopied bed. A special circular chamber, built for Gala, has extraordinary acoustics which turn every sound into a whisper. Out on the patio, olive trees are stuck into gigantic tea-cups and a stuffed boa and a statue of the Michelin Man overlook the phallus-shaped swimming pool. The Torre de les Olles, newly opened to visitors, was a secondary art studio in the garden with audio-visuals depicting Dalí and Gala in the 1960s and 1970s.

Platja de l'Almadrava, near Roses (left); medieval monastery in the Citadel (right)

Roses

Roses has been inhabited since earliest times, and there are countless megalithic monuments scattered in its vicinity. Now it's a big, modern, family-friendly resort, spread along fabulous sandy beaches.

La Ciutadella Despite Roses' long history, the city preserves few historic monuments with one notable exception: the star-shaped Citadel (La Ciutadella). These huge fortified walls, erected in the 16th century, once contained the original nucleus of Roses, before it was destroyed by the French and the new city grew up in its present location. Grassy ruins are all that survive, now transformed into a beautiful park. There is also an excellent modern museum which illustrates the city's remarkable history with audio-visual displays.

Beaches and dolmens Modern Roses is spread out behind a long, sandy beach with shallow waters. It also has a large marina, and all kinds of facilities for water sports. There are more wonderful bays around the coast, including Cala Montjoi, Almadrava and Canyelles. The tourist office has a leaflet on hikes in the region, including a megalithic route which takes in some of the ancient dolmens in the area. Roses is also on the fringes of two magnficent natural parks: the Cap de Creus natural park (▷ 67), with glorious hikes and natural scenery, and the Parc Natural de l'Aiguamolls de l'Empordà (▷ 74–75), an outstanding refuge for wetland birds.

 THE BASICS

www.roses.cat
H3
Avinguda de Rhodes 77–79, tel 902 103 636
SARFA bus from Girona and other points along the Costa Brava
Good

HIGHLIGHTS

● La Ciutadella
● Sunbathing on the beaches
● Exploring surrounding coves
● Hiking to megalithic monuments

More to See

CASTELLÓ D'EMPÚRIES

www.castello.cat

Castelló d'Empúries has a clutch of splendid monuments which date back to the Middle Ages. Grandest of all is the Basilica of Santa Maria, with a finely sculpted portal and a sublime Gothic interior. The town's substantial Jewish community was expelled in 1492, but is recalled in some of the street names—Carrer dels Jueus and Carrer del Call.

➕ G3 ℹ️ Plaça Jaume I, tel 972 15 62 33 🍽️ Numerous cafés and restaurants (€–€€€) 🚌 SARFA bus from Figueres, Girona and other places

EMPURIABRAVA

www.empuriabrava.cat

Empuriabrava is the world's largest residential marina complex, built in the 1960s. It has a permanent population of about 8,000, which swells 10-fold during the peak summer season. The town was built around a network of canals, and most residences have direct access to the water. There is a large marina, a commercial section bursting with shops, cafés, restaurants and other services, and an aerodrome with a flying club and skydiving centre.

➕ G3 ℹ️ Avinguda Pompeu Fabra s/n, tel 972 45 08 02 🍽️ Numerous cafés and restaurants (€–€€€) 🚌 SARFA bus from Figueres, Girona and other places

L'ESCALA

www.lescala-empuries.com

L'Escala has developed into a very popular tourist resort, with a huge marina and endless ranks of apartment buildings. It is famous throughout Spain for its anchovies, caught by the local fleet and hand-cured using methods dating back to the time of the Greeks. The anchovy is celebrated in the Museu de l'Anxova i de la Sal, and in the annual Festa de la Sal, held in early September.

➕ H4 ℹ️ Plaça de les Escoles 1, tel 972 77 06 03 🍽️ Numerous cafés and restaurants (€–€€€) 🚌 SARFA bus from Girona, Figueres and other places ♿ Few

Basilica of Santa Maria, Castelló d'Empúries (left); the coast around L'Escala (above)

FIGUERES

www.figueres.cat

The big draw in Figueres is the Teatre-Museu Dalí (▷ 70–71), but the town has a handful of other attractions. A stroll down the Rambla brings you to the Museu de l'Empordà (www.museuemporda. org), with its hotchpotch collection of paintings, ancient artefacts and medieval art. You can scramble up to the 18th-century Castell de Sant Ferran (www.castillosanfernando. org), one of the largest fortresses in Europe. Or visit the toy museum (Museu del Joguet de Catalunya; www.mjc.cat).

✚ F3　🚹 Plaça del Sol s/n, tel 972 50 31 55
🍽 Numerous cafés and restaurants (€–€€€)
🚆 To Figueres from Girona and Barcelona
🚌 SARFA bus from Girona and other places

LLANÇÀ

www.llanca.net

Llançà is a pretty, low-key fishing village-cum-resort, popular with Catalan families. It has an attractive little old quarter a couple of kilometres inland, with a cluster of old monuments overlooking the central Plaça Major. The modern town spills down to the harbour where the fishermen sell their catch on the quays at 4.30pm every day except Monday. The port is overlooked by Es Castellar headland, topped with the remnants of a medieval tower. There are scores of enchanting coves to explore along this stretch of coastline, and a sandy beach.

✚ H2　🚹 Carrer Camprodon 16–18, tel 972 38 08 55　🍽 Numerous cafés and restaurants (€–€€€)　🚆 To Llançà from Girona and Barcelona　🚌 SARFA bus from Girona, Figueres and other places　♿ Few

PERALADA

www.peralada.org

Peralada is a medieval village of honey-coloured stone. Its castle, begun in the 11th century, was transformed in the 19th century into an elaborate, French-style folly. It is the setting for the prestigious annual Festival Internacional de

The belltower and church on Plaça Major in Llançà

The 18th-century Castell de Sant Ferran in Figueres

Música de Peralada (mid-July to mid-August). The 11th-century cloister of Sant Domenèc is all that survives of a once-extensive medieval monastery, famous for its elaborately carved capitals which depict everything from biblical stories to gruesome medieval tortures. The town is now best known for its wines (▷ 83).

🔢 F3 ℹ️ Plaça Gran 7, tel 972 53 80 06 🍴 Numerous cafés and restaurants (€–€€€) 🚌 SARFA bus from Girona, Figueres and other places ♿ Few

EL PORT DE LA SELVA
www.elportdelaselva.cat
El Port de la Selva is spread around a wide bay on the northern flanks of the Cap de Creus. The region is a paradise for anyone interested in outdoor activities, with hiking paths, and coves for swimming, snorkelling and diving. The town is also a magnet for windsurfers and kitesurfers. Two exceptional long-distance walking paths converge here—the GR11 and the GR92.

🔢 H2 ℹ️ Carrer Illa 13, tel 972 38 71 22 🍴 Numerous cafés and restaurants (€–€€€) 🚂 To Llança from Girona and Barcelona, then local bus 🚌 SARFA bus from Girona, Figueres and other places ♿ Few

PORTBOU
http://webspobles.ddgi.cat/sites/portbou/default.aspx
Portbou, on the French frontier, was once a very busy border town. In 1995, the Schengen Accord threw open European borders, and deprived Portbou of its raison d'être. Downhill, out of sight of the train tracks, the mellow little village with its plane-shaded streets curves around a gentle bay with a pebbly beach. It has become a delightful, low-key resort, and is very popular with both French and Catalan families.

🔢 G1 ℹ️ Passeig Lluis Companys s/n, tel 972 12 51 61 🍴 Numerous cafés and restaurants (€–€€€) 🚂 To Portbou from Girona and Barcelona 🚌 SARFA bus from Girona, Figueres and other places ♿ Few

Looking down over the bay of Portbou, on the border with France

A Walk Around Cap de Creus

Enjoy the dramatic scenery of the Cap de Creus in this walk, which takes in the historic lighthouse. Bring sufficient water with you.

DISTANCE: 8km (5 miles) **ALLOW:** 3 hours

START

END

PORTLLIGAT
🚌 H2 🚌 SARFA bus

❶ From the car park at Portlligat, follow the signs for the 'Camí vell a Cap de Creus' (old path to Cap de Creus). Continue for 1km (0.5 miles), then fork right at the next sign for the Camí Vell.

❷ Keep walking until you reach the delightful cove of Guillola, with wooden boats pulled up on to the pebbly shore. In summer, there is a *xiringuito* (beach hut) where you can pick up refreshments. Walk between two houses to reach the tarmac road.

❸ After about 400m (440 yards), take the dirt path to the right. Follow this snaking path through the rocky terrain, admiring the magnificent scenery and passing three stone bridges, until the path rejoins the tarmac road.

PORTLLIGAT

❻ Return to Portlligat, following the same route.

❺ From the swimming hole, scramble up to the lighthouse, El Far Cap de Creus (▷ 67). There's a bar-restaurant next to it, with a panoramic terrace.

❹ Don't take the tarmac road, but follow the small path which leads left to the Coua de l'Infern (Cave of Hell), a stunning swimming hole. The name comes from the fact that the waters appear a deep vermilion in the dawn light. Outside the peak season, you might have it to yourself; in summer, it is usually packed with children.

Shopping

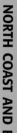

ADRIÀ BARÓ

This bakery specializes in some of the most delicious treats from the Empordà area. They make their own *bunyols de l'Empordà* (little puffs of cream-filled pastry) at Easter, but best of all are the *taps de Cadaqués*, sponge cakes which are eaten as an afternoon snack or flambéed with rum as a dessert.

✚ H3 ✉ Carrer Bellcaire 4, Cadaqués ☎ 972 25 87 55

BONES HERBES

Herbolaris (herbalists) are a fixture in all Catalan towns, and this shop sells the usual selection of dried herbs to cure all ills—great for a cold or tummy ache. It also sells natural soaps, perfumes and beauty products, as well as Catalan honeys.

✚ F3 ✉ Carrer Besalú 7, Figueres ☎ 972 67 41 35

LA BOTIGA DEL CELLER

El Castillo de Peralada is one of the biggest wine-producers in the Empordà region, and this shop-cum-tasting area gives you a chance to try some of their award-winning wines and cavas. At the top of the spectrum are the Ex Ex, Finca Garbet and Gran Claustro ranges, but even the most basic wines—such as the Roc and Blanc de Blancs—offer superb value.

✚ F3 ✉ Carrer Sant Joan 23, Peralada ☎ 972 53 85 03

SES MINVES

Ses Minves stocks a wide range of gift items, from coffee-table books and travel guides to art supplies and a selection of paintings featuring local scenes. It also sells elegant shawls and scarves, scented candles, embroidered cushions and toys.

✚ H3 ✉ Carrer Miranda s/n, Cadaqués ☎ 972 25 83 74

NICE DAY THINGS

Part of a small chain, this shop offers a fabulous range of contemporary fashion and accessories for women, including some very stylish summer dresses, bikinis and swimsuits. The styles are quirky but very wearable, and natural fabrics predominate.

POTS AND PANS

The terracotta dishes and pots *(cassoles)* seen in most tapas bars and restaurants make ideal gifts. They are sold in most *ferreteries* (hardware stores), markets and even supermarkets. Foodies might also like the large, flat paella pans (also called 'paella'). Or look for a classic Catalan wine jar, or *porró*, a glass pitcher with a long spout out of which wine spurts in a long arc. It takes practice to get it right, so don't wear your best clothes first time you try it.

✚ F3 ✉ Carrer Girona 6, Figueres ☎ 972 51 07 97

OLEA SÁTIVA

Empordà olive oil is just as prized locally as the more famous Empordà wines, and enjoys its own D.O.P. (Denominació d'Origen Protegida). Pick up some of the 'green gold' at this local producer, which also sells a small range of soaps and beauty products containing olive oil.

✚ F3 ✉ Carrer Requesens 9, Peralada ☎ 972 53 85 17

EL RACÓ DELS CONTES

This bookshop in L'Escala has a wonderful range of titles, including a reasonable selection in English and other languages. There is a large section dedicated to children's books, and the shop often arranges special events, such as storytelling for kids (usually in Catalan).

✚ H4 ✉ Plaça Victor Català, L'Escala ☎ 972 77 09 88

TECNOBICIS

www.tecnobicis.com
The Costa Brava is a popular region for cycling holidays. This shop sells all kinds of bikes, as well as bike-related equipment, clothes and accessories. There's also an excellent repair service.

✚ F3 ✉ Carrer Sant Pau 131, Figueres ☎ 972 67 41 02

Entertainment and Activities

AL CARAI

This hugely popular bar in L'Escala has DJs, a small dance floor and occasional live gigs. On balmy summer nights, it can get packed.

✚ H4 ✉ Camí Ample 3, L'Escala ☎ 972 77 10 40 🕓 Fri–Sat 11pm–3.30am; daily in high season

CAN SORT

www.cansort.com

These stables offer riding lessons, outings on horseback, riding holidays and summer camps for kids (with lessons in English). They also rent out country cottages and apartments. Can Sort is about 15 minutes from L'Escala and the beaches.

✚ F4 ✉ Carretera Báscara-Sant Mori, Km 2.8, Bàscara ☎ 972 56 03 35

CAP DE CREUS CENTRE IMMERSIÓ

www.cir-roses.com

This diving centre runs courses suitable for all levels in the pristine and protected waters of the Cap de Creus. It also offers boat rides around the headland, with daily departures in summer.

✚ H2 ✉ Carrer Pinto Martínez Lozano 9, Llançà ☎ 972 12 00 00

DISCOTECA CHIC DELUXE

www.chicdeluxe.com

One of several massive discos in and around Roses, this one has four dance floors, an outdoor terrace and a pool. As well as DJs, there are live acts, club dancers and singers, and special theme parties throughout the summer.

✚ H3 ✉ Carretera de Roses s/n, Roses ☎ 972 25 70 52 🕓 Fri–Sat 11pm–5am; daily in high season

L'HOSTAL

http://lhostal.com

Dalí himself designed the logo for this legendary jazz club in Cadaqués, which is full of dripping candles and paintings. Mick Jagger is among the celebrity visitors who have danced here in the past. Although entrance is free, drinks are very expensive, so try and come when there's a live gig. It gets incredibly busy during the summer, particularly at weekends.

EMPORDÀ WINES

The Greeks introduced the vine to the Empordà region more than 2,500 years ago. Now, it has its own D.O. (*denominació d'origen*) and produces more than 6.5 million litres a year. Whites, rosés and sweet dessert wines are all produced in the Empordà, but it is becoming best known for its elegant, full-bodied reds. New bodegas have sprung up and are gaining increasing recognition for the region. For more information check out www.doemporda.com.

✚ H3 ✉ Carrer Passeig 8, Cadaqués ☎ 972 25 80 00 🕓 Daily 11am–5am

KAYAK DEL TER

www.kayakdelter.com

This company offers canoe and kayak tours along the River Ter, ideal for birdwatchers (some sections of river close during the spring nesting season), and for families, who can choose a Canadian-style canoe which takes two adults and two children.

✚ F5 ✉ Carrer Costa Brava s/n, Colomers ☎ 662 159 469

LA PLACETA DE LA MURALLA

This lively, local pub in the heart of Sant Pere Pescador is a good place to come for a few beers, perhaps watch the football and, if you're hungry, tuck into the chunky sandwiches. It's popular with all ages, from fashion-conscious teenagers, to families with young kids.

✚ G4 ✉ Carrer Mar 15, Sant Pere Pescador ☎ 972 52 03 71 🕓 Daily 12pm–1am

TEATRE EL JARDÍ

www.figueres2009.cat

The charming, early 20th-century theatre in Figueres hosts a wide range of events, from classical theatre and circus performances to opera and modern jazz.

✚ F3 ✉ Carrer Forn Nou 9, Figueres ☎ 972 50 19 11

Restaurants

PRICES

Prices are approximate, based on a 3-course meal for one person.

€€€   over €45
€€   €25–€45
€   under €25

1869 (€)

This elegant tapas bar has a terrace overlooking the port, and serves a wide range of baguette sandwiches (flautas), tapas and simple meals.
✚ H4 ✉ Carrer del Port 11, L'Escala ☎ 972 77 68 88 🕐 Daily lunch and dinner

ES BALUARD (€€€)

www.esbaluard-cadaques.net
Es Baluard specializes in Catalan delicacies using fresh local fish. Try the outstanding suquet (fish stew), prepared with monkfish and prawns.
✚ H3 ✉ Riba Nemesi Llorens s/n, Cadaqués ☎ 972 25 81 83 🕐 Lunch and dinner; closed Sun dinner, Mon and Nov to mid-Feb

CA L'HERMINDA (€€)

www.herminda.com
Although there are more imaginative dishes on the menu, it's best to stick to the traditional favourites, such as arròs caldoso amb bogavant (a rice dish, prepared with a lobster broth).
✚ H2 ✉ Carrer Illa 7, El Port de la Selva ☎ 972 53 83 01 🕐 Lunch and dinner; closed early Jan–Feb, Wed dinner and Thu in low season

CAL NUN (€€)

Overlooking the port, this tall, thin fisherman's cottage has been turned into a restaurant but still has the feel of a private home. The menu features the day's catch, usually simply prepared over a grill and served with a chunk of lemon.
✚ H3 ✉ Plaça Port Ditxós 6, Cadaqués ☎ 972 25 88 56 🕐 Lunch and dinner; closed Sun dinner and Mon

CAL SAGRISTÀ (€€)

Cal Sagristà serves delicious, Empordan cuisine prepared with the freshest local ingredients and accompanied by a short but well-chosen wine list featuring the best Peralada wines. Try the excellent bacallà, salt cod, a Mediterranean classic.

CATALAN TAPAS

Tapas are not part of Catalonia's gastronomic tradition. Local bars always provide snacks, but these tend to be fairly simple offerings, such as platters of cheese, ham and charcuterie accompanied by country bread rubbed with tomato. However, there are several bars in the region which provide all the staple tapas, from patates braves (chunks of fried potato with a spicy sauce) to thick, potato omelette (truita in Catalan, tortilla in Spanish).

✚ F3 ✉ Carrer Rodona 2, Peralada ☎ 972 53 83 01 🕐 Lunch and dinner; closed Mon dinner and Tue

CAN CALILLO (€€)

This classic seafood restaurant offers two kinds of cuisine: you can choose from the more elaborate tasting menu (menú de degustació), comprising five or six plates of adventurous dishes, or go for the catch of the day, which will be simply prepared a la planxa (on the grill) to preserve all its succulent freshness. There is also great tapas.
✚ H3 ✉ Carrer Pi I Sunyer 24, Roses ☎ 972 25 37 82 🕐 Lunch and dinner; closed Sun dinner and Mon

CAN FORNELLS (€€)

Can Fornells has a range of Catalan dishes. Among the house specialities are Galician-style octopus served with a dash of paprika, and cod with aïoli. There's a great set-price lunch menu on weekdays.
✚ H3 ✉ Carrer Trinitat 85, Roses ☎ 972 25 42 00 🕐 Daily lunch and dinner; closed mid-Sep to mid-Jun

CAP DE CREUS (€)

The old lighthouse guardkeeper's house has been converted into a simple bar-restaurant where you can dine on local seafood or genuine Indian curries. There are simple rooms and self-

catering accommodation for rent.

⊕ J2 ✉ Carrer Faro, Cap de Creus ☎ 972 19 90 05 🕐 Daily lunch and dinner, but may close erratically

CASTELL 4 (€€)

You can eat tapas in the bar on the ground floor, or head to the dining rooms on the upper floors for more substantial fare. If you want a change from seafood, there's a good range of chargrilled meats, including *cochinillo* (suckling pig).

⊕ F3 ✉ Pujada de Castell 4, Figueres ☎ 972 51 01 04 🕐 Daily lunch and dinner; closed 3 weeks Jun–Jul and 2 weeks in Jan

KORPILOMBOLO (€€)

Korpilombolo serves fresh, sophisticated Mediterranean dishes with an imaginative twist. The tuna carpaccio comes with apple vinaigrette and wasabi 'ice cream', and desserts include tomato bread with chocolate. Book in advance.

⊕ H4 ✉ Camí Ample 40, L'Escala ☎ 972 77 32 95 🕐 Lunch and dinner; closed Sun dinner, Mon and mid-Dec to mid-Jan

LA LLAR DE PAGÈS (€€)

www.lallardepages.com
The menu features updated versions of Empordà classics, such as scallops with local sausage, or venison with a port sauce. The foie gras is made by the chef, and features in several elaborate dishes.

⊕ F2 ✉ Carrer Alt 11, Capmany ☎ 972 54 91 70 🕐 Lunch and dinner; closed Mon–Tue, dinner Sun–Thu and 3 weeks in May

MIRAMAR (€€€)

The Miramar has won a Michelin star for its impressive, contemporary Catalan cuisine. Seafood features prominently in signature dishes such as oyster tartare with caviar. Push the boat out and try the tasting menu (*menú de degustació*, €75).

⊕ H2 ✉ Passeig Marítim s/n, Llançà ☎ 972 38 01 32 🕐 Lunch and dinner; closed Sun dinner and Jan

RAFA'S (€€€)

Rafa's has no terrace or fancy decoration or even a menu: just the finest

FERRAN ADRIÀ

Ferran Adrià is one of the most famous chefs on the planet and his restaurant, El Bulli, in Roses, with three Michelin stars, is regularly voted the best in the world. It will be closing for two years from early 2012, and will open in 2014 as part of a foundation which will provide 25 culinary scholarships each year. Booking a table is unlikely to get any easier as currently there are half a million requests for fewer than 8,000 places.

fresh seafood straight from the sea. If the owner doesn't like what he sees at the fish market, he doesn't open.

⊕ H3 ✉ Carrer Sant Sebastià 56, Roses ☎ 972 25 40 03 🕐 Lunch and dinner; closed Mon

RESTAURANT EMPORDÀ (€€€)

This restaurant uses superb fresh produce, prepared in recipes which combine Mediterranean, French and Empordan influences. Go for the *menú del mercat* (€38.65), which might include tender local lamb with tomato and onion confit, or the *marinera de peixos*—a selection of the freshest fish.

⊕ F3 ✉ Avinguda Salvador Dalí 170, Figueres ☎ 972 50 05 62 🕐 Daily lunch and dinner

RESTAURANT MONESTIR DE SANT PERE DE RODES (€)

This restaurant in the monastery of Sant Pere de Rodes has a huge, picture window with views over the bay. The set menu (€13 weekdays, €15 weekends), has simple but tasty local dishes, or you can go for the more elaborate *Menu Especial* (€30).

⊕ H2 ✉ Monestir de Sant Pere de Rodes, El Port de la Selva ☎ 972 19 42 33 🕐 Lunch, dinner only available Jul and Aug by previous arrangement

This chapter takes in the southernmost delights of the Costa Brava, from family-friendly resorts like Blanes, to chic little Tossa de Mar hugging a perfect bay. Inland is the handsome market town of Vic, spread around a tremendous arcaded square.

The South Coast and Beyond

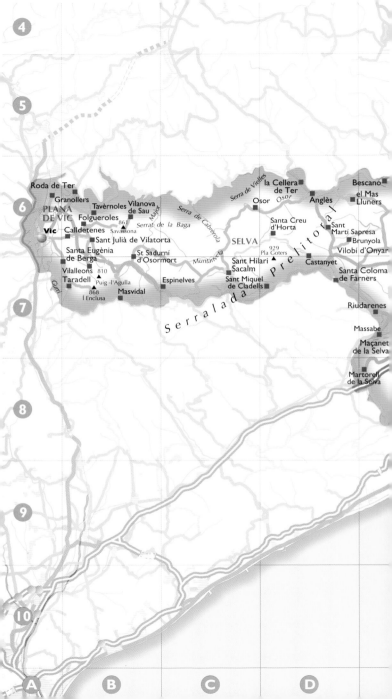

Montfullà

Vilablareix

Castellar
de la Selva

Sant Mateu
de Montnegre

Quart

406
Carreres

Daró

Sant Pol

Aiguaviva

Fornells de
la Selva

Sant Cebrià de Lledó

Vilar

Riudellots
de la Selva

Santa Pellaia

Puig d'Arques
530

Llambilles

Serra les Gavarres

Calonge

Sant Andreu
Salou

A-7

Cassà de la Selva

Serinyà

Puig Aldric
421

Romanyà
de la Selva

St Daniel

la Fosca

Caldes de
Malavella

Bruguera

Bell-lloc

Sant Antoni de Calonge

Palamós

Benaula

145
St Maurici

Llagostera

Santa Cristina
d'Aro

Solius

**Castell
d'Aro**

**Platja d'Aro
(Castell-Platja
d'Aro)**

Vidreres

Reclar

Sant Llorenç

d

**Sant Feliu
de Guíxols**

S'Agaró

Cala sa Conca

Platja de Sant Pol

Cartellà

Pins

Sant Grau

Canyet

Punta de Garbí

Terrafortuna

e

Puig de
les Cadiretes
519

Cala de Salionç

els Pantans
de Montbarbat

S

Salionç

Cap Pentiner

311
Montbarbat

Lloret Blau
les Alegries

Pola-Giverola

Cala Bona

Santa Maria
de Llorell

Tossa de Mar

Sant Pere
del Bosc

Cap de Tossa

Santa Cristina

Martossa
Canyelles

Lloret de Mar

l'Estació

Blanes

Platja de Boadella

Platja de Blanes

Punta de Tordera

0   10 km

0   5 miles

E   F   G   H

Blanes

HIGHLIGHTS

● Exploring the old quarter
● Watching the trawlers return to the fishing port
● Coastal walks

TIPS

● The Pinya de Rosa tropical gardens are quieter and less well known than Marimurtra, with splendid coastal views.
● In July, the beaches and Sa Palomera make a stunning backdrop for the international fireworks festival, Els Focs de Blanes.

The Costa Brava officially begins at Blanes, where the giant rock of Sa Palomera announces the southernmost point of the celebrated coastline. Although the village has developed into a sprawling resort, it hasn't forgotten its roots, and trawlers still bring back the day's catch to the fishing harbour.

Old quarter The narrow lanes behind the port are the historic heart of Blanes. A daily market takes place on the Passeig de Dintre, with stalls heaped high with produce from the surrounding fields and orchards. Fish stalls line Carrer de la Verge Maria, known simply as 'El Portal', which leads to Plaça de la Verge Maria, flanked by Gothic arches where the original fish market was held. Steep steps lead up to the

Clockwise from far left: The Castell de Sant Joan is a good vantage point for a sweeping vista of Blanes and its beach; the Castell's belltower; cacti at the Jardí Botànic Marimurtra, just above the town; fishing boats in the harbour; climb Sa Palomera for some of the best views of the town; tomatoes at the daily produce market

parish church and the palace of the viscounts of Cabrera, built between the 14th and 15th centuries but badly damaged after the Spanish civil war. There's a superb vantage point over the town from the lofty Castell de Sant Joan, an 11th-century castle. Near the castle is the clifftop Jardí Botànic Marimurtra (www.marimurtra.cat), one of the oldest and finest botanic gardens on the Mediterranean.

Beaches and water sports The beaches of Blanes are among the best on the Costa Brava, and include the long family-friendly strands of the Platja de Blanes and the Platja S'Abanell, as well as idyllic coves like Cala de Sant Francesc. There are outstanding facilities for every imaginable water sport, including sailing, snorkelling, diving and kayaking.

THE BASICS

www.visitblanes.net
🚏 E8
ℹ️ Passeig Catalunya 2, tel 972 33 03 48
🕐 Jun–Sep daily 10–8; Oct–May 10–6
🚌 SARFA and Barcelona Bus from Barcelona and Girona. There are local bus services within Blanes
🚆 From Barcelona to Blanes station 2km (1.2 miles) from town centre
♿ Few

Sant Feliu de Guíxols

HIGHLIGHTS

- Museu de la Vila
- Modernista mansions on the Passeig del Mar
- Fishing boats in the harbour
- Lazing on the beaches
- Hiking the coastal paths to quiet coves

TIP

- For fabulous coastal views, climb up to the 18th-century hermitage of Sant Elm.

Sant Feliu de Guíxols is a handsome seaside town, with a smattering of Modernista mansions, a colourful fishing harbour and some glorious beaches. It remains pleasingly low-rise and low-key.

Monastery and museums Sant Feliu grew up around a ninth-century Benedictine monastery. The Gothic parish church was built over the ruins and preserves an austere but beautiful interior. Adjoining buildings, mostly constructed in the 18th century, now contain museums and exhibition spaces, including the Museu de la Vila (city history museum). Work is under way to expand the complex to display the 19th- and 20th-century Catalan paintings from the art collection amassed by Carmen Thyssen-Bornemisza. The new museum opens in 2011.

Clockwise from far left: The remains of the Benedictine monastery; the Moorish-style Nou Casino de la Constància, with its arches and turrets; the beach at Sant Feliu is a wide arch of sand with a harbour at its north end; fishing is still an imporant industry in town; colourful houses in the Old Town; the market hall has art deco touches

Modernista mansions From the 19th century until the 1930s, Sant Feliu grew rich on the export trade in cork. Merchants displayed their wealth with dazzling Modernista mansions. The most extravagant mansion is the Casa Patxot at No. 40 Passeig del Mar. You can have a drink at the 19th-century Nou Casino de la Constància, better known locally as the Casino dels Nois ('the boys' casino'). Nearby, the Toy Museum (Museu de la Joguina, www.museudelajoguina. cat) is housed in a splendid 19th-century mansion with Modernista touches.

Port and beaches The sandy arc of Sant Feliu's long beach culminates in the old port. The old coastal smuggling paths *(camins de ronda)* wriggle around the coast, linking the town with numerous coves and tiny beaches.

THE BASICS

www.guixols.net

➕ G7

ℹ️ Plaça del Mercat, Casa Gareta, tel 972 82 00 51

🚌 TEISA and SARFA buses from Girona and Barcelona

♿ Few

❓ A miniature train tours the town in summer

Tossa de Mar

TOP
25

HIGHLIGHTS

- La Vila Vella
- The Chagall paintings in the Museu Municipal
- El Far de Tossa

TIP

- Tossa holds its weekly market on Thursday morning.

Tossa de Mar has been the most glamorous resort of the southern Costa Brava since Ava Gardner came here in the 1950s. The medieval village spills down the hillside to a perfect bay.

La Vila Vella This is Tossa de Mar's most celebrated landmark, a tiny but perfectly preserved medieval village which was enclosed by walls against the threat of pirates. The Museu Municipal occupies the 14th-century Casa Falguera, built for an early governor, and has an excellent collection of modern and contemporary art. Highlights include Marc Chagall's *El Violinista Celeste*: Chagall was seduced by Tossa's extraordinary light and spent two summers here in the early 20th century. This lofty headland was once crowned by a

The ruins of the old Gothic church of Sant Vicenç (top left); the Mediterranean Lighthouse Interpretation Centre in the old lighthouse (below left); a fortified medieval village looks down onto the beach at Tossa de Mar (below)

castle, but it was replaced in the 19th century with a lighthouse, El Far de Tossa, which still functions, and also contains an interpretation centre on Mediterranean lighthouses. There are fabulous views from this promontory.

Around the bay One of the earliest mansions built outside the walled village was 16th-century Can Ganga, which now contains the Museu Etnogràfic (ethnographic museum). By the 18th century, when the parish church of Sant Vicenç was built, the town centre had shifted downhill from the Vila Vella. The church now dominates the old fishermen's quarter. The coastline around Tossa de Mar is spectacularly beautiful, pocked with little coves like the Cala Pola and the Cala Giverola to the north, or the Cala d'en Carlos and the Cala Figuera to the south.

THE BASICS

www.infotossa.com

⊞ F8

🛈 Avinguda del Pelegrí 25, Edifici La Nau, tel 972 34 01 08

🚍 SARFA bus from Barcelona and Girona

🚆 To Blanes from Barcelona, then local bus

♿ Few

Vic: Museu Episcopal and Catedral

HIGHLIGHTS

● Romanesque belltower
● The cloister
● Sert's extraordinary murals in the cathedral
● Romanesque murals
● Gothic paintings
● Mediterranean antiquities

TIP

● The museum has a great programme of family-friendly activities; take a look at the website.

Vic was once the seat of a powerful bishopric, and its splendid cathedral reflects the city's historic importance. The wealthy bishops accumulated a fabulous collection of religious art, now housed in a sleek, purpose-built museum.

Cathedral interior The first cathedral to occupy this spot was established in the 11th century, but was torn down in the 18th century to make way for the present neoclassical building. However, the Romanesque belltower was incorporated into the new design, along with the delicate cloister and the crypt. The interior is dominated by blazing murals in scarlet and gold by the Catalan painter Josep M. Sert, who was also responsible for the murals in New York's Rockefeller Center. The paintings

Clockwise from left: Murals by Catalan artist Josep Maria Sert adorn the walls; a wealth of Catalan religious art, stretching back almost a thousand years, is housed in the cathedral; the present neoclassical building dates from 1803

were destroyed during the Spanish Civil War, but Sert returned to repair the damage, and died only days after they were inaugurated anew in 1945. He is buried in the cloister.

Museum highlights Over the centuries, the cathedral amassed a superb collection of religious art, enlarged in the 19th century by artefacts discovered during excavation of Vic's Roman temple. In 2002, the collections were moved to a glassy new building next to the cathedral. The artworks span more than a millennium, and include Romanesque murals from local churches and Gothic paintings. The Roman artefacts include Mediterranean antiquities gathered by enthusiastic amateurs in the 19th century: look for the 10th-century BC Egyptian sarcophagus and mummy.

THE BASICS

www.museuepiscopalvic.com

➕ A6

✉ Plaça Bisbe Oliba 3

☎ 938 86 93 60

🕐 Apr–Sep Tue–Sat 10–7, Sun 10–2; Oct–Mar 10–1, 3–6, Sat 10–7, Sun 10–2

🍴 Several cafés and restaurants nearby (€–€€€)

🚌 SARFA and Barcelona Bus run direct services from Girona and Barcelona

🚆 To Blanes from Barcelona, then local bus

♿ Good

💲 Moderate

❓ Guided visits (free) Sat morning at 11.30

Vic: Plaça Major and Market

Café on the Plaça Major (left); the basket market (middle); the facade of Casa Comella (right)

THE BASICS

www.victurisme.cat
➕ A6
✉ Carrer Ciutat 4
☎ 938 89 26 37
🚆 Train from Barcelona
♿ Few
❓ See Vic by Segway: ask for information at the tourist office

HIGHLIGHTS

● Browsing in the Plaça Major's old-fashioned shops
● Historic houses around the Plaça Major
● El Mercadal

TIPS

● Vic is famous for its *embutits* (cured sausages), particularly *fuet*.
● Come on a Tuesday if you want to avoid the crowds.
● The Saturday market is much bigger.
● Palm Sunday (Diumenge dels Rams) sees the city host the Mercat del Ram, a traditional livestock market.

Flanked with arcades and overlooked by historic mansions, Vic's vast Plaça Major makes a theatrical setting for its celebrated market, El Mercadal, which takes place every Tuesday and Saturday.

Historic mansions The houses which enclose the Plaça Major form a harmonious ensemble nowadays, but they date back to different periods. The oldest is the Casa Beuló, which has preserved much of its original Gothic structure. Look for the Casa Tolosa and the Casa Moixó, which each retain baroque elements. There's a sprinkling of modest Modernista mansions, including the Casa Comella, with sgraffito decoration swirling across the facade. For all their disparate styles, the mansions are gracefully knitted together by the ranks of arcades which enclose the square.

El Mercadal The Plaça Major has been the social and commercial heart of the city since ancient times. The twice-weekly market, El Mercadal, has been held here for a thousand years, with stalls selling everything from pottery to sausages cramming the enormous square and filling the ancient arcades. It may seem chaotic at first sight, but in fact the market is carefully laid out, with all the fresh fruit and vegetables occupying one corner, the flowers another, and the sausage-makers (for whom Vic is so well known) yet another. The centre of the square is filled with stalls selling everything from fake FC Barça T-shirts to paella pans.

More to See

CASTELL D'ARO
www.platjadaro.com
Although now known principally for its famous beach resort, Platja d'Aro (▷ 100), Castell d'Aro preserves a charming, if minuscule, old quarter, dominated by the much-restored 11th-century castle which gave the town its name. The castle is now a cultural centre which hosts temporary exhibitions and contains a curious doll museum, the Museu de la Nina, with more than 300 dolls from around the world.
➕ G7 🛈 Carrer Mossèn Cinto Verdaguer 4, tel 972 81 71 79 🍴 Several cafés and restaurants (€–€€€) 🚌 SARFA bus from Girona and Barcelona ♿ Few

Museu de la Nina
✉ Passeig Lluís Companys 1 🕐 Summer Mon–Fri 6–9pm, Sat–Sun 11–1, 6–9; winter Sat–Sun 11–1, 5–7 💲 Free

LLORET DE MAR
www.lloretdemar.org
Lloret de Mar, with its high-rise hotels, pub-lined streets and fabulous beaches, has been geared towards package tourism since the boom began in the 1950s. However, the former fishing village has more to offer, not least a spectacular coastline filled with delightful coves, the remains of ancient Iberian settlements, and a cemetery with lavish Modernista tombs. The botanic gardens of Santa Clotilde, breathtakingly set high on a cliff top, offer dazzling views over the coastline, and there's a fantastic cliff walk to Tossa de Mar (▷ 94–95).
➕ F8 🛈 Avinguda de les Alegries 3, tel 972 36 57 88 🍴 Numerous cafés and restaurants (€–€€€) 🚌 SARFA bus from Girona and Barcelona 🚆 Train to Blanes, then local bus ♿ Few

PALAMÓS
www.palamos.cat
Many resorts on the Costa Brava have forgotten their seafaring past, but maritime traditions are still going strong in Palamós. It boasts the third-largest commercial port in Catalonia, with a substantial fishing

The Modernista tile roof of Lloret de Mar's church of Sant Roma

The fishing harbour at Palamós

fleet which you can watch returning every afternoon around 4pm. At the fish market, look for the Palamós prawns which are served in local restaurants. You can find out all about the town's long maritime history at the entertaining Museu de la Pesca (www.museudelapesca. org), near the port. In summer, the seafront is lit up with fireworks for the Nit de Sant Joan (23 June), a fire festival which has its roots in pre-Christian traditions. Coastal walks *(camins de ronda)* lead to exquisite coves like Cala S'Alguer and Cala Estreta.

➕ H7 ℹ Passeig del Mar s/n, tel 972 60 05 50 🚌 SARFA bus from Girona and other places ♿ Few

PLATJA D'ARO

www.platjadaro.com

Platja d'Aro is a big, modern resort famous for its gorgeous beaches and intense summer nightlife. It is a lively residential resort, with more apartment buildings than hotels, and is very popular with Catalan visitors. The Platja Gran is the main beach, a vast sweep of golden sands, but some beautiful, quieter and smaller beaches can be found at Cala del Pi, Cala sa Conca and Cala dels Canyers. A coastal walk leads to S'Agaró (▷ below).

➕ G7 ℹ Carrer Mossen Cinto Verdaguer 4, tel 972 81 71 79 🚌 SARFA bus from Girona and other places ♿ Few

S'AGARÓ

www.platjadaro.com

The exclusive residential enclave of S'Agaró came about when a wealthy industrialist bought land in the 1920s, and commissioned Catalan architect Rafael Masó i Valenti to create the luxurious dwellings in traditional style. There are currently about 60 residences in the original community. The legendary Hostal de la Gavina overlooks the community, and the charming beach of Sant Pol.

➕ G7 ℹ Carrer Mossen Cinto Verdaguer 4, tel 972 81 71 79 🚌 SARFA bus from Girona and other places ♿ Few

Activities at Platja d'Aro (above); a cove between Sant Pol and Cala sa Conca (right)

A Drive From Tossa de Mar

This drive takes in the most dramatic stretch of road on the southern Costa Brava: between Tossa de Mar and Sant Feliu de Guíxols.

DISTANCE: 32km (20 miles)   **ALLOW:** 3 hours (including stops) one way

 START   **END**

TOSSA DE MAR

+ F8   SARFA bus from Girona and Barcelona

TOSSA DE MAR

1 After a stroll around the charming resort of Tossa de Mar, gather some picnic supplies and water, then head north from Tossa de Mar on the GI-682, following signs for Sant Feliu de Guíxols.

6 The GI-682 heads inland through pine forest before reaching Sant Feliu de Guíxols (▷ 92–93). Explore the attractive resort before returning back along the corniche to Tossa de Mar.

2 The road immediately begins to climb, then twist and turn through luxuriant groves of pine and cork. There are several *miradors* (viewing spots) along the road.

5 Return to the corniche road, and continue north towards Sant Feliu de Guíxols. You will soon arrive at the small resort of Canyet de Mar, a collection of villas and apartment buildings. Just beyond Canyet de Mar is the Platja Rosamar, an attractive beach and a good stop for a dip.

3 The russet cliffs plunge down to enchanting little bays with turquoise waters, and the road regularly swoops down to curve around a picturesque cove. Stop at the Cala Pola (park near the Sant Pol campsite), about 5km (3 miles) from Tossa de Mar, and head through the campsite to the beach for a short stroll.

4 Continue along the corniche until you reach Salionç, then turn left, heading uphill towards the Santuari de Sant Grau. After 5km (3 miles), you will reach a 19th-century sanctuary set in woods: there are great views over the coast and some shady picnic spots nearby.

Shopping

CANSALADERIA-XARCUTERIA SOLÀ

One of three celebrated charcuterie shops on the splendid Plaça Major, this has been making Vic's famous cured sausages since the 19th century. All kinds of sausages—*fuet*, *llonganissa*, *xoriço* among them—are produced. Choose a couple to slice up with some country bread and a ripe tomato for a delicious and quintessentially Catalan picnic.

✚ A6 ✉ Plaça Major 31, Vic ☎ 938 86 02 19

CELLER D'OSONA

This wine shop has a huge range of wines, cavas and liqueurs, but the emphasis is firmly on local producers. As well as the most famous Catalan bodegas, you'll find plenty of choices from among less well-known but eminently interesting small wineries.

✚ A6 ✉ Carrer Sant Fidel 3, Vic ☎ 938 86 00 60

ESPARDENYERIA D'ESPART

This shop (established in 1866) stocks a wide range of traditional *espardanyes*, from the simplest slip-on kind, which are perfect for the beach, to slightly more elaborate wedge-heeled affairs for women, which look great with linen trousers. They also have the traditional flat-soled espadrilles tied with two-

tone ribbons, traditionally used when dancing the stately Catalan round dance, the *sardana*. There's a cute selection for children, including some embroidered with flowers.

✚ E8 ✉ Carrer Jaume Ferrer 14, Blanes ☎ 972 35 55 92

FANGSESC

Barcelona-born sculptor Francesc Antón Martrus Narbot creates all kinds of unusual designer ceramics, from huge abstract sculptures to pretty pendants in organic shapes.

✚ E8 ✉ Carrer Esperança 71, bajos A, Blanes ☎ 972 33 02 93

GALERIA JOAN PLANELLAS

www.galeriajoanplanellas.com
Tossa de Mar's extra-ordinary light and dramatic natural beauty still attract many artists.

ESPARDANYES

Espardanyes (espadrilles) are rope-soled canvas shoes which have been worn in Catalonia since at least the 14th century. They have become fashionable in the last few decades and even top fashion houses such as Chanel have produced their own designer versions. Several specialist shops still make them using traditions handed down through generations.

There are several galleries showing their work, but this is probably the best known.

✚ F8 ✉ Carrer Sant Pere 10, Tossa de Mar ☎ 972 34 25 11

ÎLE AUX TRÉSORS

A good range of bathing costumes, beachwear, towels, flip-flops and sun hats can be found here.

✚ G7 ✉ Carrer Creu 37, Sant Feliu de Guíxols ☎ 972 32 83 76

INTERSPORT MARQUES

www.intersport-marques.com
This is a large sports shop, which is handy if you require outdoor equipment during your stay. The stock ranges from fishing tackle and camping gear to clothing and snorkels, and they also have plenty of toys and games to keep kids happy at the beach.

✚ F8 ✉ Carrer Sant Pere 56, Lloret de Mar ☎ 972 36 69 47

MONT-FERRANT

www.montferrant.com
This award-winning bodega, established in 1865, claims to be the oldest company dedicated to producing cava in Spain. It makes a range of cavas, of which the best is probably the Mont Ferrant Gran Reserva. Visits must be booked in advance.

✚ E8 ✉ Carrer Abat Escare 1, Blanes ☎ 934 19 10 00

Entertainment and Activities

BLANES-SUB

www.blanes-sub.com
Blanes-Sub offers dives and courses to suit everyone from beginners to the more advanced divers. Equipment is available for rent and the dives are directly from the beach, or from boats.
🗺 E8 ✉ Explanada del Port, Blanes ☎ 972 33 40 04 or 646 96 20 56

CASINO LLORET DE MAR

www.casino-lloret.com
As well as the usual gambling activities, Lloret's casino offers dinner shows and concerts. Passports and smart dress are required; no under-18s.
🗺 F8 ✉ Carrer dels Esports 1, Lloret de Mar ☎ 972 36 61 16 🕐 Jun–Jul daily 7pm–4am, Aug daily 6pm–5am; Sep Sun–Thu 6pm–4am, Fri–Sat 6pm–5am

CLUB DE GOLF COSTA BRAVA

www.golfcostabrava.com
This prestigious golf club has a demanding 18-hole golf course. It offers private lessons, and you can dine in a 19th-century farmhouse, now the club house.
🗺 G7 ✉ Santa Cristina d'Aro ☎ 972 83 70 55

CLUB DE VELA DE BLANES

www.cvblanes.cat
The sailing school at Blanes has a range of courses for all levels, and is particularly well geared towards children.
🗺 E8 ✉ Explanada del Port, Blanes ☎ 972 33 05 52

DISCOTECA CLUB & LOFT

www.discoloft.com
Platja d'Aro is the main nightlife hub of the central Costa Brava. This huge nightclub is very fashionable and is open throughout the year.
🗺 G7 ✉ Avinguda S'Agaró 120, Platja d'Aro ☎ No tel 🕐 Sat midnight–5am, daily in high season

DISCO TROPICS

This massive disco on three floors has four different spaces playing different music. In summer, it hosts all kinds of theme parties, including an infamous foam party.

KIDS' ACTIVITES

If sun, sea and sand ever pall, there are several theme parks and water parks you can visit. These include Waterworld, in Lloret de Mar (www.waterworld.es); Marineland, in Palafolls (www.marineland.es); Aquabrava, near Roses (www.aquabrava.com); and Aquadiver, in Platja d'Aro (www.aquadiver.com). Go-karts are also popular along this coast, with karting tracks in Blanes, Roses, Palamós, L'Escala and Empuriabrava.

🗺 F8 ✉ Avinguda Just Mariés 35, Lloret de Mar ☎ 972 36 42 14 🕐 Thu–Sat 11pm–5am, daily in high season

DOFIJET BOATS

www.dofijetboats.com
Dofijet Boats has two boat services along the southern Costa Brava. The 'Blue Flying' line is a ferry service between Blanes and Palamós, with stops at most resorts and coves, while glass-bottomed boats ply the 'Blue Eye' line, which runs between Lloret de Mar and Tossa de Mar. The boats only run between June and October and may be cancelled due to bad weather.
🗺 E8 ☎ 972 35 20 21

JAZZ CAVA

www.jazzcava.com
This low-lit subterranean jazz bar with stone walls and a tiny stage hosts regular concerts and jam sessions. Come in May to enjoy the citywide Jazz Festival.
🗺 A6 ✉ Rambla dels Montcada s/n, Vic ☎ 93 889 2505 🕐 Thu–Sat 10.30pm–3am. Closed end Jul to mid-Sep

ZOOM ELECTRIC CLUB

Small but hugely popular dance club, with DJs playing electro-pop to a hip young crowd.
🗺 F8 ✉ Carrer Ponent 30, Lloret de Mar ☎ No tel 🕐 Fri–Sat midnight–5am

Restaurants

PRICES

Prices are approximate, based on a 3-course meal for one person.

€€€	over €45
€€	€25–€45
€	under €25

CAFÈ DE L'ORFEÓ (€)

Popular with a young crowd, who come for the bargain tapas, salads and tasty grilled meats.

⊞ A6 ✉ Plaça Santa Cecilia s/n, Vic ☎ 938 85 07 47
🕓 Daily lunch and dinner

CAN CARLUS (€€–€€€)

www.cancarlus.com
Can Carlus serves tasty and unusual Tossenca specialities such as *cim i tomba* (fish stew with potatoes, onions and tomatoes) or *faves ofegades* (broad beans with herbs and bacon).

⊞ F8 ✉ Carrer Portal 20, Tossa del Mar ☎ 972 34 08 04 🕓 Daily lunch and dinner

CAN TARRANC (€€–€€€)

www.cantarranc.net
Classic Catalan dishes are on the menu, exquisitely presented and prepared with fresh seasonal ingredients. Try the *suquet de rape*, a rich fish stew made with monkfish and clams.

⊞ E8 ✉ Carretera Blanes-Tordera Km 2, Blanes ☎ 937 64 20 37 🕓 Lunch and dinner; closed Mon–Fri Oct–May, Mon Jun–Sep and mid-Jan to mid-Feb

CASA TERRASSANS (€)

Some of the best traditional tapas in town is served at this old-fashioned café-bar. The house speciality is *calamars* or *sepia a la romana* (battered squid or octopus rings), but the menu includes classics like *patates braves* (fried chunks of potato with a mildly spicy sauce) and *gambas al ajillo* (prawns cooked with garlic).

⊞ E8 ✉ Passeig de Dintre 31, Blanes ☎ 972 33 00 81
🕓 Daily lunch and dinner

EL CAU DEL PESCADOR (€€)

www.caudelpescador.com
This restaurant specializes in seafood. Go for the fresh fish baked in a salt crust to preserve the juiciness of the flesh,

CHARCUTERIE

The pig is revered throughout Spain, where vast amounts of ham and other pork products are consumed annually. Catalonia is particularly famous for its *embutits*—different kinds of sausage, made with meat mixed with various herbs and spices and stuffed (traditionally, at least) into intestines. The market town of Vic is renowned for its *llonganissa* and *fuet*, both made with pork, bacon and black pepper, formed into long, thin sausage shapes and hung to cure.

or the *coca* (flat bread) topped with anchovies.

⊞ G7 ✉ Carrer Sant Domènec 11, Sant Feliu de Guixols ☎ 972 37 18 69
🕓 Daily lunch and dinner

EL CELLER DE LA PUNTAIRE (€€)

www.elcellerdelapuntaire.com
El Celler uses organic produce as much as possible, and specializes in fresh Mediterranean fare with an Italian accent. There's a good selection of vegetarian dishes. On weekday lunchtimes, there's a set lunch for €12.50.

⊞ E8 ✉ Carrer Mirador de S'Auguer, Blanes ☎ 972 35 90 97 🕓 Lunch and dinner; closed Sun dinner, Mon and Tue

LA CUINA DE CAN SIMON (€€€)

www.lacuinadecansimon.es
La Cuina's roots are in traditional Catalan recipes, elegantly brought up to date by young chef Xavier Lores. The restaurant has a Michelin star.

⊞ F8 ✉ Carrer Portal 24, Tossa de Mar ☎ 972 34 12 69 🕓 Lunch and dinner; closed Sun dinner, Mon and Tue in low season, 2 weeks in Nov and 2 weeks in Feb

DISASTER CAFÉ (€€)

At this theme restaurant you'll experience volcanoes and other scary surprises as the evening progresses. It's not suitable for very small children, or anyone with a

heart problem. The food is pretty standard—pizzas, fried chicken, *croquetes* (potato croquettes).

⊞ F8 ⊠ Carrer Francesc Layret 9, Lloret de Mar ☎ 972 36 02 50 🕐 Daily lunch and dinner

DUES SOLES (€)

Dues Soles doesn't serve full meals, but there's an excellent range of tapas, from simple *pa amb tomàquet* (▷ below) served with local *fuet* (cured sausage) to more elaborate fare.

⊞ A6 ⊠ Carrer Dues Soles 6, Vic ☎ 938 81 62 91 🕐 Lunch and dinner; closed Tue

FISHOP (€€€)

www.grupofishop.com
Fishop serves a fabulous, if rather pricy, mixture of fresh Mediterranean and Japanese specialities, including sushi. In the fish shop section, an extraordinary variety of fish is laid out on ice: pick whatever looks good and the kitchen will prepare it to order.

⊞ G7 ⊠ Galeries San Lluís 22, Platja d'Aro ☎ 972 81 66 74 🕐 Daily lunch and dinner

FONDA CAN SETMANES (€–€€)

www.fondacansetmanes.com
This traditional restaurant serves well-priced, traditional Catalan cuisine, including wonderful rice and seafood dishes. The set menu at lunchtimes is a bargain at under €10

weekdays, and under €15 at weekends.

⊞ E8 ⊠ Carrer Antiga 26, Blanes ☎ 972 33 00 11 🕐 Daily lunch and dinner

LA GALERA (€€€)

The old-fashioned La Galera specializes in fish—literally plucked only hours before from the sea. Everything is so fresh that it needs nothing more than a few minutes on the grill *(a la planxa)*. House specialities include Palamós prawns, famed for their sweetness.

⊞ H7 ⊠ Carrer Mauri Vilar 21, Palamós ☎ 972 31 51 78 🕐 Daily lunch and dinner

EL JARDÍN (€€)

The wide-ranging menu here offers everything from paella to steaks, as well as tapas and *racions*.

⊞ F8 ⊠ Carrer Areny 9, Lloret de Mar ☎ 972 36 66 82 🕐 Daily lunch and dinner

---

PA AMB TOMÀQUET

Catalan cuisine is famous around the world, thanks to super chefs such as Ferran Adrià of El Bulli, but the most characteristic Catalan dish is *pa amb tomàquet* (bread with tomato). It's nothing more than a slice of country bread rubbed with garlic and fresh tomato, then drizzled with olive oil and a pinch of salt, but it's very tasty, and is the perfect accompaniment to *embutits* (charcuterie) and cheese.

LEVANT (€–€€)

This Italian restaurant is a good option for families, with a long menu that includes child-friendly salads, pastas, pizzas, crêpes and ice creams.

⊞ G7 ⊠ Avinguda S'Agaró, Platja d'Aro ☎ 972 81 75 37 🕐 Daily lunch and dinner

LA TAULA (€€)

The house speciality is *bacallà* (cod), prepared here in six different ways. The salads are delicious, particularly the one with goat's cheese, and the desserts are home-made.

⊞ A6 ⊠ Plaça Miquel Clariana 4, Vic ☎ 938 86 32 29 🕐 Lunch and dinner; closed Sun dinner, Mon and 2 weeks in Aug

VILLA MÁS (€€€)

Spectacularly fresh seafood and a superb setting make this restaurant an outstanding dining option. There's a huge terrace, as well as a pretty, light-filled dining room to try the sophisticated Catalan cuisine. The wine list is exceptionally good and features one of the finest selections of Burgundy wines in Spain. A set lunch is available for €22 on weekdays. The (free) parking is a real boon in the height of the summer season.

⊞ G7 ⊠ Passeig Sant Pol 95, Sant Feliu de Guíxols ☎ 972 82 25 26 🕐 Lunch and dinner; closed Mon and Dec

The Costa Brava offers a wide range of accommodation, from rustic country inns to chic beachside spa hotels. Book months in advance for a place in August, when prices double or even triple.

Introduction

Whether you want a five-star spa resort on the beach or a simple country inn, the Costa Brava has it. Note that many coastal properties close in the winter, usually from November until Easter. The best deals can almost always be found on the internet: try websites such as www.hotels.com, www.destinia.com and www.lastminute.com.

Types of Accommodation

Spanish hotels are classified, regularly inspected and awarded 1 to 5 stars *(estrellas)*. These stars refer to facilities and don't take into account charm or service. *Hostales* are often hard to distinguish from small hotels and can be better value for money. They are graded from 1 to 3 stars: a 3-star *hostal* is generally on a par with a 2-star hotel. *Pensiones* are family-run establishments with simple rooms that may or may not have private bathrooms. In high season, you may be required to take meals in your hotel. There are lots of self-catering options, from luxury villas and inexpensive holiday apartments on the coast, to country cottages inland. Good websites to check out include www.costabrava.org, www.toprural.com and www.catalunyaturisme.com.

Rural Tourism

Inland options can be found just a short drive from the coast, so you can enjoy the beaches, but retreat from the hubbub in the evenings. For self-catering accommodation in the country, try www.toprural.com, www.casesruralesgirona.com or www.gironarural.org. If you prefer hotels, try www.innsofspain.com and www.rusticae.es.

PARADORS

The state-run hotels, *paradors*, are often located in spectacular historic buildings such as monasteries or castles. There are two on the Costa Brava. The modern *parador* in Aiguablava sits on a clifftop overlooking a stunning little cove, while the more traditional one in Vic is next to a huge lake. See www.parador.es.

There's a wide variety of accommodation to choose from and it's classified and graded by the government

Budget Hotels

CAN MAS

www.canmas.net
This 17th-century *masía* has a choice of pretty bedrooms, each named for a fruit grown on the property, or self-catering apartments. It's close to the beaches and the ruins in Empúries.
➕ G4 ✉ Carretera de Sant Pere Pescador a Sant Martí d'Empúries, Sant Pere Pescador ☎ 972 52 02 58

CAN MASSA

Can Massa has rustic accommodation, great country breakfasts and a friendly welcome. It's a perfect base for cycle touring, with numerous bike trails in the area.
➕ F5 ✉ Carrer Vell, La Pera ☎ 972 48 83 26

HOTEL BLAU MAR

www.hotelblaumar.com
Hotel Blau Mar has bright, airy bedrooms overlooking a courtyard. There's a swimming pool and a good restaurant, and the nicest rooms—worth splashing out the extra for—have terraces with sea views. In August, prices jump into the next category.
➕ H3 ✉ Carrer Massa d'Or 21, Cadaqués ☎ 972 15 90 20 🕐 Closed early Nov–early Mar

HOTEL CAL TET

www.caltet.com
Modest, but spotless rooms all stylishly decorated, delightful service and a central location make this a great budget hotel.
➕ H5 ✉ Carrer Santa Anna 38, L'Estartit ☎ 972 75 11 79

HOTEL EL CAU DEL PAPIBOU

www.hotelelcau.net
The rooms here are decorated in rustic style with creamy bedspreads and wooden furnishings. The restaurant serves delicious modern Catalan cuisine, and it's just a 20-minute drive to some splendid little coves.
➕ G5 ✉ Carrer Major 10, Peratallada ☎ 972 63 40 18

HOTEL LA MUNTANYA

www.hotelmontecarlo llafranc.com
Book well in advance to bag one of the very well-priced rooms at this simple, modern hotel. Functional rather than

CAMPING

Camping can be a good budget option if you are travelling with children. The Catalan government publishes an annual directory (€6, available in local bookshops), or you can find listings online at www.catalunyaturisme.com or www.costabrava.org.

charming, it's a good bet if you plan to be out and about all day and want a reasonably priced base.
➕ H6 ✉ Carrer Cesàrea 2, Llafranc ☎ 972 30 04 04 🕐 Closed early Nov–early Mar

HOTEL ROSA

http://fondacaner.com
This little inn offers impeccable rooms—some with jacuzzi baths—at a bargain price. Breakfast is served at its excellent local restaurant (Fonda Caner, ▷ 62), just across the street.
➕ H6 ✉ Carrer Pi i Ralló 19, Begur ☎ 972 62 30 15 🕐 Closed early Nov–early Feb

MAS FUSELLES

www.masfuselles.com
This country house is great for families, with playgrounds, animals (including ponies) and special weekend activities. Everyone will enjoy the pool and jacuzzi.
➕ E5 ✉ Mas Fuselles s/n, Cornellà del Terri ☎ 972 59 48 41

PENSIÓN BELLMIRALL

www.grn.es/bellmirall
Tucked away in Girona's medieval quarter, Pensión Bellmirall is an enchanting guest house with just a handful of rooms set around a courtyard in a 14th-century building. Bring earplugs—the cathedral bells echo!
➕ e2 ✉ Carrer Bellmirall 3, Girona ☎ 972 20 40 09

Mid-Range Hotels

PRICES

Expect to pay between €100 and €200 per night for a double room in a mid-range hotel.

AC PALAU DE BELLAVISTA

www.ac-hoteles.com
A new contemporary five-star hotel with all modern amenities close to Girona's old town. Geared towards business travellers, it offers great weekend deals that can often push it down into the budget category.
 Off map at f4 ✉ Pujada Polvorins 1, Girona ☎ 872 08 06 70

ALMADRABA PARK

www.almadrabapark.com
This huge, modern hotel sits on a stunning promontory on the border of the Cap de Creus nature reserve. The best rooms have magnificent sea views, and there's a pool, tennis court and an excellent restaurant serving contemporary Mediterranean cuisine.
✚ H3 ✉ Platja de l'Almadraba, Roses ☎ 972 25 65 50 ⏰ Closed early Nov–Mar

HOTEL AATU

www.hotelaatu.net
The Aatu offers stylish rooms, two pools and a terrace restaurant. The owners can arrange everything from golf to a balloon ride.

✚ G5 ✉ Carretera Vullpellac, Peratallada ☎ 617 464 914

HOTEL AIGUACLARA

www.aiguaclara.com
You'll need to book months in advance for this exceptional little hotel. The restaurant serves superb local cuisine. Guests appreciate the charming welcome and thoughtful extras.
✚ H6 ✉ Carrer Sant Miquel 2, Begur ☎ 972 62 29 05 ⏰ Closed Jan to mid-Feb

HOTEL ARCS DE MONELLS

www.hotelarcsmonells.com
The main building is set in a 14th-century hospital, but most rooms are in an ultra-modern annexe. There's a small pool and a good restaurant. Prices soar in August.
✚ G6 ✉ Carrer Vilanova 1, Monells ☎ 972 63 03 04 ⏰ Closed 2 weeks in Dec

THE CATALAN *MASÍA*

The Catalan *masía* is a traditional country house or farmhouse, usually built of stone, and almost always in a rural location. Some date back to the Middle Ages. Many had fallen into ruin by the early 20th century, but now they are highly sought-after. Most have been sumptuously restored, either as private homes, or as boutique hotels and luxurious inns.

HOTEL DIANA

www.diana-hotel.com
This classic hotel occupies a listed Modernista mansion. The rooms are plain and functional, but the courtyard (where breakfast is served) and lavish salons are a delight.
✚ F8 ✉ Plaça Espanya 6, Tossa de Mar ☎ 972 34 18 86 ⏰ Closed early Nov–Mar

HOTEL LLEVANT

www.hotel-levant.com
The rooms vary considerably in size and comfort, and it's worth paying the supplement for those with a terrace and a sea view. Breakfast is served in a dining room overlooking the bay.
✚ H6 ✉ Carrer Francesc de Blanes 6, Llafranc ☎ 972 30 03 66 ⏰ Closed early Nov–early Dec

HOTEL MAS PAU

www.maspau.com
The restaurant here is one of the finest in Catalonia, but Mas Pau also has elegant rooms and suites set in a handsomely renovated, 16th-century manor.
✚ F3 ✉ Carretera Figueres a Besalú, Avinyonet de Puigventós ☎ 972 54 61 54 ⏰ Closed early Jan to mid-Mar

HOTEL MAS TAPIOLAS

www.sallashotels.com
This sumptuous country hotel, in a peaceful, wooded valley, has a pool in the gorgeous gardens,

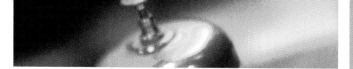

an excellent spa and a fine restaurant. Activities in the region include golf, cycling and horse-riding.

G7 ✉ Carretera C65 km 7, Veinat de Solius s/n, Santa Cristina d'Aro ☎ 972 31 42 08

HOTEL SANT JOAN

www.hotelsantjoan.com
Hotel Sant Joan is set amid lush gardens just inland from the beaches. Service is outstanding, and the rooms are warmly decorated and comfortable. There's a swimming pool, and the nearest beach is just 1km (0.5 miles) away.

H7 ✉ Avinguda de la Llibertat 79, Palamós ☎ 972 31 42 08 Closed Nov–Jan

HOTEL TAMARIU

www.tamariu.com
This old-fashioned seafront hotel sits in the middle of one of the prettiest bays on the Costa Brava. Rooms are simple, but spotlessly clean, and some have balconies overlooking the bay. Choose a room on the upper floors in peak season: those on lower floors can be noisy.

H6 ✉ Passeig del Mar 2, Tamariu ☎ 972 62 00 31 Closed mid-Dec to Feb

HOTEL DEL TEATRE

www.hoteldelteatre.com
This immaculate boutique hotel makes a perfect base for exploring the medieval villages of the Baix Empordà. Each of

the seven rooms is decorated with creamy fabrics and pale walls, and amenities include Bang&Olufson TVs and music systems.

H6 ✉ Plaça Major s/n, Regencós ☎ 972 30 62 70 Closed Nov to mid-Mar

HOTEL TRIAS

www.hoteltrias.com
Hotel Trias is a chic boutique hotel and restaurant with gleaming minimalist rooms right on the seafront. The fashionable mixture of original details and contemporary design has made it a favourite with stylish city-dwellers looking for a weekend break, so book well in advance.

H7 ✉ Passeig del Mar, Palamós ☎ 972 60 18 00

MOLÍ DEL MIG

www.molidelmig.com
A 16th-century mill has been exquisitely restored to create this ultra-chic

hotel. Minimalist designer furnishings contrast with the stone walls and wooden beams, and bedrooms are divided between the mill and a contemporary annexe. There's an outstanding restaurant, a pool in the gardens and a new spa and wellness area.

H5 ✉ Camí del Mig, Torroella de Montgrí ☎ 972 75 53 96 Closed early Jan to mid-Feb

EL RACÓ DE MADREMANYA

www.turismoruralgirona.com
This 16th-century *masía* has been sumptuously converted into a chic little boutique hotel. There are two pools (one with sea water) in the gardens, and massages and other beauty treatments can be arranged. Not suitable for children under 12.

F5 ✉ Carrer Processó 1, Madremanya ☎ 972 49 06 49

SANT ROC

www.santroc.com
Set amid Mediterranean pine forest on a cliff overlooking a little bay, the Sant Roc is a delightful family-run hotel. There are shady gardens, a path leading directly down to the beach and a restaurant with sea views. It's worth paying extra for a room with a terrace.

H6 ✉ Plaça Atlàntic 2, Calella de Palafrugell ☎ 972 61 42 50 Closed early Nov–early Mar

Luxury Hotels

HOTEL AIGUABLAVA

This seaside hotel is set in gardens with a seawater pool. Try to get a room with a terrace overlooking the sea. The hotel restaurant is outstanding, and there's a less expensive bistro and barbecue area.

 H6 ✉ Platja de Fornells, Begur ☎ 972 62 20 58 ⏱ Closed mid-Oct to mid-Mar

HOTEL LES COLS PAVELLONS

The Michelin-starred restaurant at Les Cols is a magnet for gourmets, but fans of contemporary architecture will want to spend the night in one of the futuristic, glassy 'pavilions'. The astonishing crystal cubes provide an experience akin to floating in air in a zen-like space.

C4 ✉ Mas Les Cols, Avinguda Les Cols 2, Olot ☎ 699 81 38 17 ⏱ Closed 2 weeks in Jan

HOTEL EL FAR DE SANT SEBASTIÀ

www.elfar.net
El Far occupies a renovated 18th-century inn next to the Sant Sebastià lighthouse. There are just nine luxurious rooms and suites and a restaurant.

H6 ✉ Muntanya de Sant Sebastià, Llafranc ☎ 972 30 16 39 ⏱ Closed early Jan–early Feb

HOTEL LA MALCONTENTÁ

www.lamalcontentahotel.com
La Malcontenta is surrounded by lush, landscaped gardens, with an enormous pool, and the stylish rooms are beautifully decorated with a mixture of rustic and contemporary furnishings.

H7 ✉ Paratge del Torre Mirona, Platja de Castell 12, Palamós ☎ 972 31 23 30

HOTEL MAS VILALONGA PETIT

www.masvilalongapetit.com
This 18th-century country house in the quiet hills of Les Gavarres is surrounded by huge gardens. It is seriously dedicated to peace and as such it's a child-free zone. The restaurant has a romantic terrace.

F6 ✉ Veïnat Verneda 21, Cassà de la Selva ☎ 972 46 19 93

HOTELS FOR FOODIES

Some hotels on the Costa Brava are just as famous for their restaurants as they are for their accommodation. Among the best options are: Hotel Aiguaclara and Hotel Mas Pau (▷ 110); Molí del Mig (▷ 111); Hotel Les Cols Pavellons, Hotel Aiguablava, Hotel El Far de Sant Sebastià and Hotel Peralada (▷ 112).

HOTEL PERALADA WINE SPA AND GOLF

www.hotelperalada.com
Hotel Peralada overlooks an 18-hole golf course. It has its own golf school and pro-shop, and there's a wine spa where you can pamper yourself with relaxing beauty treatments using products made with local wines or grapes. There is also an excellent gourmet restaurant.

F3 ✉ Carrer Rocabertí s/n, Peralada ☎ 972 53 88 30

MAS FALGARONA

www.masfalgarona.com
This country hotel has 10 rooms and suites. Golf fans can choose from the 10 courses in the area, while sun-seekers lounge by the pool or book a massage.

F3 ✉ Carrer Lles, Avinyonet de Puigventós, near Figueres ☎ 972 54 66 28

MAS DE TORRENT

www.mastorrent.com
Perhaps the most luxurious accommodation on the Costa Brava with a huge pool set in landscaped gardens. The spa has a wide range of treatments. Choose from the *masía*, or more modern accommodation with private terraces. The restaurant is superb.

H6 ✉ Carrer Afueras s/n, Torrent ☎ 972 30 32 92 ⏱ Restaurant closed early Jan–early Feb. Spa closed Mon in winter

This section is full of useful information on planning a trip to the Costa Brava, and finding your way around once you're there. We've included some language tips and historical pointers.

Planning Ahead

When to Go

The Costa Brava enjoys year-round sunshine. The coastline is packed in July and August, when the heat can be intense. The inland regions, however, usually provide a shady retreat from the coastal chaos. Note that many businesses close up in the winter in the coastal resorts.

TIME

L Spain is one hour ahead of GMT, six hours ahead of New York and nine hours ahead of Los Angeles.

AVERAGE DAILY MAXIMUM TEMPERATURES

JAN	FEB	MAR	APR	MAY	JUN	JUL	AUG	SEP	OCT	NOV	DEC
13°C	14°C	17°C	19°C	21°C	25°C	27°C	27°C	25°C	22°C	20°C	17°C
55°F	57°F	63°F	66°F	70°F	77°F	81°F	80°F	77°F	72°F	68°F	63°F

Spring (mid-March to mid-June) is a beautiful time to visit, particularly if you enjoy hiking and birdwatching.

Summer (mid-June to mid-September) is very warm, but rarely gets uncomfortably hot, except in late July and August. In late summer, the rice and grapes ripen in the fields.

Autumn (mid-September to mid-December) is cooler, but usually still sunny. From October, many coastal resorts close up.

Winter (mid-December to mid-March) is a great way to enjoy the wild scenery without the crowds, although it can get surprisingly chilly.

WHAT'S ON

Every town and village hosts an annual *festa major* in honour of its patron saint. The Costa Brava tourist board has a comprehensive list (www.costabrava.org).

December/January *Nadal* (Christmas): Celebrations start in early December and end on 5 January with the *Cavalcada de Reis*, or Procession of the Three Kings, who bring the children sweets and presents.

February/March *Carnestoltes* (Carnival): Children get dressed up and parade through their towns and villages.

March/April *Pasqua* (Easter): Includes the unusual *Dansa de Mort* (Dance of Death), held in Verges on Holy Thursday.

Sant Jordí (23 Apr): Catalonia celebrates its patron saint.

May *Carroussel* and *Festes de Primavera:* This spring festival is held in Palamós, and features parades of lavishly decorated floats and *correfocs* (fire-running).

June *Nit de Sant Joan* (24 Jun): On the night before the feast of Sant Joan, all of Catalonia explodes with fireworks and bonfires in a fire-themed festival.

July/August Crowds gather in early July in Calella de Palafrugell to listen to the *Cantanada d'Havaneres*, old sea shanties brought from the Caribbean more than a century ago. Nearby towns host smaller *havaneres*. *Music Festivals* The summer months are packed with superb music festivals.

September *La Diada* (11 Sep): Catalonia's national day.

November All Saints' Day (1 Nov): Catalans honour the dead. Families eat traditional foods and relatives visit cemeteries to leave flowers.

Costa Brava Online

www.costabrava.org
Official regional tourism website. Available in several languages.

www.catalunyaturisme.com
Catalan government's tourist website. Also a good source of information on Catalan culture and traditions. Available in several languages.

www.gencat.cat/parcs
Information on Catalonia's natural parks and nature reserves. Catalan and Spanish only.

www.innsofspain.com
Small and reliable hotel-booking agency, which focuses on charming accommodation.

www.renfe.es
Spanish national railways. English-language option available—click Seleccione su idioma.

www.wunderground.com
Accurate weather forecasting. In English.

www.quierohotel.com
Spain-based booking site, with hotels all over the country. In English.

www.parador.es
Official site of the state-run *parador* network. Special web-only offers available.

www.iberia.es
Spain's national airline. Online booking available with special offers.

www.toprural.com
A great site for *cases rurals* (country cottages) and rural hotels.

www.restaurantscostabrava.com
A selection of local restaurants. Available in Catalan, Spanish and English.

WIFI

Most hotels now offer free WiFi to guests, and increasing numbers of cafés and bars are beginning to offer it too. It's usually free if you make a purchase on the premises, although some places may charge by the hour (it's rarely more than €3 per hour). Mobile phone operators in Spain, including Movistar and Vodaphone, offer a pay-as-you-go internet service.

INTERNET CAFÉS

Internet cafés come and go all the time. You can generally find a couple of internet terminals in the *locutoris* (phone centres). Tourist offices usually provide the most up-to-date information. The following addresses might be useful:

Café de Nit
✉ Plaça del Sol 2, Figueres
☎ 972 50 12 25

Roses Ciber Centre
✉ Carrer Aragó 19, Roses
☎ 972 25 65 57

Les Gavines
✉ Passeig del Mar 15, L'Escala
☎ 972 77 33 90

Jaba Net
✉ Carrer Dídac Garrell I Tauler 10, Palamós
☎ 972 31 49 06

Getting There

ENTRY REQUIREMENTS

● Anyone entering Spain must have a valid passport (or official identity card for EU nationals). Visa requirements are subject to change, so check before making your reservations.

● Passengers on all flights to and from Spain are required to supply advance passenger information (API) to the Spanish authorities. Full names, nationality, date of birth and travel document (passport) details are required. If you book flights online, you will usually be required to provide the information at the time of booking.

CUSTOMS

● The limits for non-EU visitors are 200 cigarettes or 50 cigars or 250g of tobacco; 1 litre of spirits (over 22 per cent) or 2 litres of fortified wine, 2 litres of still wine; 50ml of perfume. Travellers under 18 are not entitled to the tobacco and alcohol allowances.

● The guidelines for EU residents (for personal use) are 800 cigarettes, 200 cigars, 1kg of tobacco; 10 litres of spirits (over 22 per cent), 20 litres of aperitifs, 90 litres of wine, of which 60 can be sparkling wine, 110 litres of beer.

AIRPORTS

Most European flights, including charter flights, arrive in Girona, the main airport for the Costa Brava. The biggest international airport is El Prat, in Barcelona, 100km (62 miles) south of Girona. For general information on all Spanish airports, go to www.aena.es, tel 902 40 47 04.

BY AIR

Girona Airport is 14km (9 miles) south of the city centre, next to the AP7/E10 *autopista*, the main highway along the Mediterranean coast and the most useful to access points along the Costa Brava. Taxis are available outside the arrival terminal and cost between €16 and €25 to the centre of Girona: for average prices to other destinations along the Costa Brava, see the airport website. There's a regular, if slow, local bus service into Girona's city centre, and SARFA buses (www.sarfa.com) and Barcelona Bus (www.barcelonabus.com) run coach services directly to the main destinations along the Costa Brava.

If you arrive at Barcelona airport, there are regular bus and train links to Girona, the main hub for bus services to the Costa Brava. There are direct buses from Barcelona's Estació del Nord bus station

(www.barcelonanord.com) for most coastal destinations. A taxi from Barcelona airport to Girona costs around €125.

BY BUS
Girona is the main transport hub for the Costa Brava. The large bus station is next to the train station on Plaça Espanya (tel 972 21 33 19), close to the old centre. International coach services arrive here from across Europe (www.eurolines.es). Local buses head out to the main coastal destinations. Figueres bus station, next to the main train station, at Plaça d'Estació (tel 902 43 23 43), is also an international destination, although not as busy as Girona. It is most convenient for bus services to destinations along the northern Costa Brava.

BY TRAIN
Girona and Figueres are the main train hubs for northern Catalonia, with high-speed services from Madrid and the rest of Spain. There are long-distance trains from Paris, Zurich, Montpellier and other destinations across Europe. By 2015, the high-speed AVE train should link Barcelona and Paris in under six hours. Local trains run from Barcelona to Blanes in the south; a regional line runs from Barcelona via Girona to Portbou on the French border. Flaçà has the nearest train station for central Costa Brava (around Begur and Pals), with daily services to Barcelona and Girona. There is a wide variety of Spanish trains, from the fast, expensive Talgo and Euromed trains to the cheaper local commuter services (*cercanías* in Spanish, *rodalies* in Catalan). For more information, or to book online, consult the website: www.renfe.es, or call 902 32 03 20.

BY CAR
The AP7/E10 *autopista* (toll motorway) runs south from the French border. This is the main highway for the Costa Brava, and continues down the Mediterranean coast of Spain. It can get very busy during the peak summer season.

Getting Around

VISITORS WITH DISABILITIES

Facilities on the Costa Brava are improving, but they are still generally poor. All modern hotels, restaurants, museums and other attractions are required to provide facilities for wheelchair-users, but older properties, apart from the most luxurious places, are rarely modernized. MIFAS (www.mifas.cat, also in English) can provide information on wheelchair-accessible bars and restaurants in the centre of Girona, and also has an online map showing wheelchair-accessible beaches.

CENTRE BTT

The Catalan government has established a network of cycle centres (Centre BTT) where visitors can rent bikes and try out some local bike trails. The centres are often found in stunning rural locations, and are well set up for cyclists of all ages and abilities. Each has an information point, which provides lists of local restaurants along the routes, as well as tips on the right route for your level of ability. www.turismedecatalunya.com/btt (also in English) has a list of the bike centres, and information on the length and difficulty of the trails.

NEED TO KNOW GETTING AROUND

BUSES

Most towns and villages along the Costa Brava are linked by bus. The biggest bus companies on the Costa Brava are SARFA (www.sarfa.com), TEISA (www.teisa-bus.com), Barcelona Bus (www.barcelonabus.com) and AMPSA (www.ampsa.org). The main hubs for bus services are Girona and Figueres, where the bus stations are located next to the train stations. The regional tourist office website, www.costabrava.org, lists all the bus companies, along with a list of their main routes. Timetables can usually be found on websites (rarely available in English), and tourist offices are very helpful. Services to smaller towns and villages, including popular tourist attractions like Pals, are very limited, with perhaps just one or two buses a day.

TRAINS

Train services are limited along the Costa Brava. Local trains (rodalies in Catalan) link Barcelona with Blanes, the southernmost resort on this stretch of coast, where you can get local buses to Lloret de Mar and Tossa de Mar. Another train line (used by slightly faster, as well as more expensive, regional and long-distance trains) runs inland from Barcelona to Girona before heading back out to the coast at Portbou, the most northerly resort of the Costa Blanca. Buses from Portbou head down the coast to Llança and El Port de la Selva. Vic and Ripoll inland can be reached directly by train from Barcelona, but not directly from Girona: if you don't have a car, it's easiest to take the bus. For timetables, see www.renfe.es, or call 902 320 320.

BICYCLES

The Catalan government has established a network of cycle centres (▷ panel), where you can hire bikes and enjoy the local scenery from signposted trails. The Baix Empordà is flat and relatively empty, and there are more demanding trails in the rugged Cap de Creus and the mountains around Ripoll. It is best to stick to cycle lanes and signposted cycle routes.

DRIVING

Car rental rates are fairly reasonable, but it pays to shop around to find the best price. Book well in advance to get a good deal in the peak season (mid-July to end-August).
Rules of the road:

● Traffic drives on the right.

● The speed limit is 50kph (31mph) in urban areas, unless otherwise indicated, and 90kph (56mph) elsewhere.

● Look for entry and exit ramps on the inside lane of dual carriageways, and left-hand turns that require you to turn into a right-hand sliproad and stop before crossing the traffic.

● A no-entry sign on the left-hand side as you exit a roundabout means stick to the right as traffic is two-way.

● *Canvi de sentit* (Catalan)/*Cambio de sentido* (Spanish) on an exit sign means that the exit allows you to reverse direction by rejoining the road on the other carriageway.

TAXIS

Taxis are plentiful in the cities and major resorts. In smaller villages, you may need to book one in advance. Taxis are required to turn on the meter in urban areas, but along the coast many will make long trips for a set price (agree a price in advance). www.costabrava.org has a list of taxi operators across the region. These include:
Taxis Girona: tel 972 22 23 23
Radio Taxi Roses: tel 972 25 30 33
Tossa de Mar: tel 972 34 05 49
L'Escala: tel 972 77 35 18

WALKING

The Costa Brava is a superb destination for walkers, with a range of trails to suit hikers of all abilities. As well as some spectacular GR routes (see box), the region has a number of nature reserves with great walking trails, including the dramatic headland of the Cap de Creus, the marshes (or *aiguamolls*) of Empordà, which are a haven for birdlife, and the green volanic hills of La Garrotxa.

MAPS

Tourist offices across the region are an outstanding source of local maps, from resort guides to leaflets describing local hikes. There are several good online maps available at www.costabrava.org. Recommended maps for those planning extensive explorations by car include those published by the Automobile Association. Sunflower publishes a good walking guide to the Costa Brava region.

GR FOOTPATHS

Several spectacular long-distance footpaths converge on the Costa Brava. The magnificent GR11 begins in Cadaqués and crosses the Pyrenees to culminate at Hondarribia in the Basque country. The GR92, which begins in Portbou by the French border, descends along the entire Mediterreanan coast.
The GR1 gives an historic overview of Catalonia, beginning next to the ancient Greek colony at Empúries and passing the monastery established by Wilfred the Hairy, in Ripoll, before culminating in the Pyrenees. Federació d'Entitats Excursionistes de Catalunya (www.feec.cat) can provide more information (in Catalan only).

Essential Facts

5 euros

10 euros

50 euros

100 euros

MEDIA

The two biggest Spanish national daily newspapers are *El País* and *El Mundo*. In Catalonia, the most important publications are *La Vanguardia* (Spanish), *El Periodico* (available in Spanish and Catalan), *Avui* (Catalan), *El Punt* (Catalan) and the *Diari de Girona* (Catalan). The monthly *Catalonia Today* is an excellent English-language newspaper, which is also available online (for a fee). International newspapers are easily available in all but the smallest towns and villages. Most hotels receive BBC, Sky and CNN, plus several other international channels. Almost every town has at least one bar where you can watch sporting fixtures on a big screen. Xtra.fm is an English-language radio station broadcasting on the Costa Brava.

MEDICINES AND HEALTHCARE

● In the case of medical emergencies, head for the emergency department *(servei d'urgencies)* of the nearest hospital. Most towns and villages have a CAP (Centre d'Attenció Primària), public health centre, some of which are open 24 hours.
● Pharmacies *(farmacies)* are indicated by an illuminated green cross; they are usually open 9.30–2 and 5–8. All post a list of *farmacies de guardia* (all-night chemists), or you can look online at www.cofgi.com/p1.php (available in several languages).
● For information on the European Health Insurance Card (EHIC), ▷ 117.

MONEY MATTERS

● Credit cards are widely accepted in all larger hotels and shops, but rarely in smaller businesses. You must show photo ID when paying with a card.
● ATMs, with instructions in several languages, are widely available, and this may be the most convenient way to withdraw euros. However, find out from your bank what the fees are for this service.

● Travellers' cheques are not widely accepted, except in the largest hotels and restaurants.

NATIONAL HOLIDAYS

1 Jan, 6 Jan, Maundy Thursday (Mar/Apr), Good Friday (Mar/Apr), 1 May, 30 May, Corpus Christi (May/Jun), 11 Sep, 12 Oct, 1 Nov, 6 Dec, 8 Dec, 25 Dec.

OPENING HOURS

● Banks: banks generally open from 8.30 to 2, Monday to Friday.

● Shops: smaller shops open from 9.30/10am to 1.30/2 then again from 4/4.30 to 8/8.30, Monday to Saturday. Larger shops, especially in the city centres, forgo the midday closing and stay open all day. Sunday trading is restricted to shops selling food and tourist-targeted retailers.

● Museums: most major museums close Sunday afternoons and Mondays. Many smaller ones open mornings only.

● Restaurants: kitchens catering for locals will rarely open before 8.30pm, though it's easy to have an early meal in the resorts and tourist areas. Some fashionable restaurants may open all day—part of a new trend in Spain.

TELEPHONES

● Public telephones take *tarjetas* (cards), available from newsstands; some also take coins. Instructions are posted in several languages, including English.

● *Locutoris* are call centres, where you make calls from a private phone booth for a very low price. Many also offer internet and fax services.

● Spain uses the GSM mobile phone system, which is compatible with most mobile phones, except those from the USA. If your phone is uncoded (ie not 'locked' into one provider) you can buy a 'pay as you go' SIM card and use it with a local provider on local rates. If not, you will pay roaming rates.

● To call Spain from the UK dial 00 34 followed by the local number. To call the UK from Spain dial 00 44, Australia 00 61 and the USA 00 1.

TOILETS

Popular beaches have portaloos. Bars generally let you use their facilities, though it's polite to buy a drink at the bar. Look for *senyores* or *homes* (men), or *senyoras* or *damas* (women).

TOURIST OFFICES

Every town and village has at least one tourist office, all well equipped and staffed with helpful, multilingual staff. Here are some central options:

● Banyoles: Passeig Darder, pesquera 10 ☎ 972 58 34 70

● Begur: Avinguda Onze de Setembre 5 ☎ 972 62 45 20

● Girona: Rambla de la Llibertat ☎ 972 226 575

● L'Estartit: Passeig Marítim s/n ☎ 972 75 19 10

● Olot: Carrer Hospici 8 ☎ 972 26 01 41

● Pals: Plaça Major 7 ☎ 972 63 61 61

● Ripoll: Plaça de l'Abat Oliba s/n ☎ 972 70 23 51

MAIL

● Stamps *(segells)* are available from tobacconists *(estancs)*.

● Post boxes are yellow and marked *correos*.

● A postcard to the UK and other European destinations costs €0.64: to the USA and Canada €0.78.

Language

There are two official languages in Catalonia: Catalan and Spanish. All local government literature, road signs and menus are in Catalan, although you'll find most things are multilingual in the main resorts. The Catalans are proud of their language, and appreciate any efforts to speak even a word or two. Spanish may be more widely spoken in some beach resorts, but Catalan predominates inland.

CATALAN

BASIC VOCABULARY

yes/no	*si/no*
please/thankyou	*si us plau/gràcies*
good morning	*bon dia*
good evening	*bona tarda*
I don't understand	*no l'entenc*
I don't speak Catalan	*no parlo Català*
left/right	*esquerra/derecha*
entrance/exit	*entrada/sortida*
open/closed	*obert/tancat*
good/bad	*bo/dolent*
big/small	*gran/petit*
with/without	*amb/sense*
hot/cold	*calent/fred*
today/tomorrow	*avui/demà*
yesterday	*ahir*
how much is it...?	*Quant costa això...?*
where is the ...?	*On es el/la...?*
do you have...?	*Tens...?*
I'd like...	*Voldría...*

NUMBERS

1	*un/una*
2	*dos*
3	*tres*
4	*cuatre*
5	*cinc*
6	*sis*
7	*set*
8	*vuit*
9	*nou*
10	*deu*
20	*vint*
30	*trenta*
40	*quaranta*
50	*cinquanta*
60	*seixanta*
70	*setanta*
80	*vuitanta*
90	*noranta*
100	*cent*
1,000	*mil*

EATING OUT

glass of wine	*un got de vi*
glass of beer	*una canya*
water (mineral)	*aigua (mineral)*
still/sparkling	*sense gas/amb gas*
coffee (with milk)	*cafè amb llet*
May I have the bill?	*El comte si us plau*
Do you take credit cards?	*Accepten targetes de crèdit?*
set dishes	*plats combinats*
smoking allowed	*es permet fumar*
no smoking	*prohibit fumar*

BASIC VOCABULARY

yes/no	*si/no*
please/thankyou	*por favor/gràcias*
good morning	*buenos días*
good evening	*buenas tardes*
I don't understand	*no entiendo*
I don't speak Spanish	*no hablo español*
left/right	*izquierda/derecha*
entrance/exit	*entrada/salida*
open/closed	*abierto/cerrado*
good/bad	*bueno/malo*
big/small	*grande/pequeño*
with/without	*con/sin*
hot/cold	*caliente/frio*
today/tomorrow	*hoy/mañana*
yesterday	*ayer*
how much is it...?	*¿cuánto es?*
where is the ...?	*¿donde está....*
do you have...?	*¿tiene...?*
I'd like...	*me gustería*

NUMBERS

1	*uno*
2	*dos*
3	*tres*
4	*cuatro*
5	*cinco*
6	*seis*
7	*siete*
8	*ocho*
9	*nueve*
10	*diez*
20	*veinte*
30	*treinta*
40	*cuarenta*
50	*cincuenta*
60	*sesanta*
70	*setanta*
80	*ochenta*
90	*noventa*
100	*cien*
1,000	*mil*

EATING OUT

glass of wine	*copa de vino*
glass of beer	*caña*
water (mineral)	*agua (mineral)*
still/sparkling	*sin gas/con gas*
coffee (with milk)	*café (con leche)*
May I have the bill?	*La cuenta, por favor*
Do you take credit cards?	*¿Aceptan tarjetas de crédito?*
set dishes	*platos combinados*
smoking allowed	*se permite fumar*
no smoking	*se prohibe fumar*

Timeline

EARLY PEOPLES

The earliest signs of human habitation in the Costa Brava region date back as much as 450,000 years, according to the most recent studies. There are numerous dolmens and other megalithic constructions, particularly around Roses and in the hills of Les Gavarres. The earliest Iberian settlement in Catalonia, settled around the 6th century BC, has been discovered near Ullastret.

575BC Greek traders establish a settlement at Empúries.

218BC The Romans arrive in Empúries and begin their conquest of Hispania.

5th century AD The region falls under Visigothic rule after the collapse of the Roman Empire.

AD711 North African armies cross the Straits of Gibraltar and sweep northwards. They conquer several important Catalan cities, including Girona around AD715.

AD785 Northern Catalonia is reconquered by Charlemagne, the Frankish Emperor, who establishes the Hispanic Marches as a buffer zone between the Christian and Muslim armies.

c.840–97 Guifré el Pilós (Wilfred the Hairy) is born. Under his leadership, a number of petty kingdoms across the Hispanic Marches are united into what will eventually become Catalunya (Catalonia).

1492 Ferdinand and Isabella, the 'Catholic Monarchs', order that all Jews convert or leave Spain.

From left: statue of Asclepius at Empúries; Roman mosaic at Empúries; the 12th-century cloisters of the Monestir de Santa Maria in Ripoll; Ferdinand and Isabella, the 'Catholic Monarchs'; heron in the Aiguamolls natural park

1659 Through the Treaty of the Pyrenees, Catalonia loses its historic territories north of the Pyrenees.

19th century Catalans head to the West Indies to make their fortunes. Those who return are called Indianos, and build lavish homes, many of which still exist.

1908 The term 'Costa Brava' is coined by local journalist Ferran Agulló.

1936–39 The Spanish Civil War. General Franco takes control of Spain.

1960s Mass tourism takes off along the Costa Brava.

1975 General Franco dies, and democracy is re-established in Spain.

1998 The Carta de Tossa is signed, pledging to respect the natural environment on the Costa Brava.

2012 The high-speed AVE train line from Madrid via Barcelona and Girona is expected to reach the French border.

ARTISTS AND THE COSTA BRAVA

The exceptional natural beauty and spectacular light drew artists to the Costa Brava long before it was 'discovered' by tourists. Marc Chagall spent two summers in Tossa de Mar, and Picasso, Miró and David Hockney are just some of the artists drawn to Cadaqués, where Salvador Dalí built his home.

THE DALÍ TRIANGLE

The most famous local resident of the Costa Brava is Salvador Dalí, the arch Surrealist, who was born in Figueres in 1904. The Theatre-Museum he created (and where he was entombed after his death in 1989) is one of the biggest attractions in Spain. The two lesser-known corners of the Dalí Triangle are the artist's enchanting home in Portlligat, and the castle he gave to his wife and muse, Gala. See www.salvador-dali.org.

Index

TWINPACK
Costa Brava

WRITTEN BY Mary-Ann Gallagher
COVER DESIGN Catherine Murray
DESIGN WORK Lesley Mitchell
INDEXER Marie Lorimer
IMAGE RETOUCHING AND REPRO Sarah Montgomery
PROJECT EDITOR Karen Kemp
SERIES EDITOR Marie-Claire Jefferies

© **AA MEDIA LIMITED 2011**

Colour separation by AA Digital Department
Printed and bound by Leo Paper Products, China

A CIP catalogue record for this book is available from the British Library.

ISBN 978-0-7495-6804-7

Published by AA Publishing, a trading name of AA Media Limited, whose
registered office is Fanum House, Basing View, Basingstoke, Hampshire
RG21 4EA. Registered number 06112600.

Front cover: AA/M Bonnet
Back cover: (i) AA/M Bonnet; (ii) AA/C Sawyer; (iii) AA/M Bonnet;
(iv) AA/M Bonnet

A04027
Maps in this title produced from map data supplied by Global Mapping,
Brackley, UK. Copyright © Global Mapping/Cartografia

The Automobile Association would like to thank the following photographers, companies and picture libraries for their assistance in the preparation of this book.

Abbreviations for the pictures credits are as follows – (t) top; (b) bottom; (c) centre; (l) left; (r) right; (AA) AA World Travel Library.

1 AA/M Bonnet; **2** AA/M Bonnet; **3** AA/M Bonnet; **4t** AA/M Bonnet; **4l** AA/M Bonnet; **5t** AA/M Bonnet; **5b** AA/M Bonnet; **6t** AA/M Bonnet; **6cl** AA/M Bonnet; **6cc** AA/M Bonnet; **6cr** AA/M Bonnet; **6bl** AA/M Bonnet; **6bc** AA/M Bonnet; **6br** AA/M Bonnet; **7t** AA/M Bonnet; **7cl** AA/M Bonnet; **7cc** AA/M Bonnet; **7cr** AA/M Bonnet; **7bl** AA/M Bonnet; **7bc** AA/M Bonnet; **7br** Howard Sayer/Alamy; **8** AA/M Bonnet; **9** AA/M Bonnet; **10t & 11t** AA/M Bonnet; **10c** AA/M Bonnet; **10b** AA/M Bonnet; **11c** AA/M Bonnet; **11b** AA/M Bonnet; **10/11t** AA/M Bonnet; **10/11b** AA/M Bonnet; **12t & 13t** AA/M Bonnet; **12tc** AA/M Bonnet; **12c** AA/M Bonnet; **12bc** AA/M Bonnet; **12b** AA/M Bonnet; **13tc** AA/M Bonnet; **13c** AA/M Bonnet; **13bc** AA/M Bonnet; **13bc** AA/M Bonnet; **14t** AA/M Bonnet; **14tc** AA/M Bonnet; **14c** AA/M Bonnet; **14bc** AA/M Bonnet; **14b** AA/M Bonnet; **15t** AA/M Bonnet; **15b** AA/M Bonnet; **16t** AA/M Bonnet; **16tc** AA/M Bonnet; **16c** AA/M Bonnet; **16b** AA/M Bonnet; **17t** AA/M Bonnet; **17tc** AA/M Bonnet; **17c** AA/M Bonnet; **17bc** AA/M Bonnet; **17b** AA/M Bonnet; **18t** AA/M Bonnet; **18tc** AA/M Bonnet; **18c** AA/M Bonnet; **18bc** AA/M Bonnet; **18b** AA/M Bonnet; **19(i)** AA/M Bonnet; **19(ii)** AA/M Bonnet; **19(iii)** AA/M Bonnet; **19(iv)** AA/M Bonnet; **20/21** AA/P Enticknap; **24l** AA/M Bonnet; **24r** AA/M Bonnet; **24/25** AA/M Bonnet; **25t** AA/M Bonnet; **25b** AA/M Bonnet; **26l** AA/M Bonnet; **26c** AA/M Bonnet; **26r** AA/M Bonnet; **27l** AA/M Bonnet; **27r** AA/M Bonnet; **28t** AA/M Bonnet; **28bl** AA/M Bonnet; **28br** AA/M Bonnet; **29t** AA/M Bonnet; **29bl** AA/M Bonnet; **29br** AA/M Bonnet; **30** AA/M Bonnet; **31** AA/M Bonnet; **32** AA/M Bonnet; **33** AA/C Sawyer; **34** AA/C Sawyer; **35** AA/M Bonnet; **38l** AA/M Bonnet; **38r** AA/M Bonnet; **38/39** AA/M Bonnet; **39t** AA/M Bonnet; **39bl** AA/M Bonnet; **39br** AA/M Bonnet; **40l** AA/M Bonnet; **40c** AA/M Bonnet; **40r** AA/M Bonnet; **41l** AA/M Bonnet; **41r** AA/M Bonnet; **42l** AA/M Bonnet; **42r** AA/M Bonnet; **43l** blickwinkel/Alamy; **43r** AA/M Bonnet; **44** AA/M Bonnet; **45t** AA/M Bonnet; **45b** AA/M Bonnet; **46l** AA/M Bonnet; **46tr** AA/M Bonnet; **46br** AA/M Bonnet; **47t** AA/M Bonnet; **47bl** AA/M Bonnet; **47br** AA/M Bonnet; **48l** AA/M Bonnet; **48c** AA/M Bonnet; **48r** AA/M Bonnet; **49l** AA/M Bonnet; **49c** AA/M Bonnet; **49r** AA/M Bonnet; **50t** AA/M Bonnet; **50bl** AA/M Bonnet; **50br** AA/M Bonnet; **51t** AA/M Bonnet; **51b** AA/M Bonnet; **52t** AA/M Bonnet; **52b** AA/M Bonnet; **53t** AA/M Bonnet; **53b** AA/M Bonnet; **54t** AA/M Bonnet; **54b** AA/M Bonnet; **55t** AA/M Bonnet; **55bl** AA/M Bonnet; **55br** AA/M Bonnet; **56** AA/M Bonnet; **57** AA/M Bonnet; **58** AA/M Bonnet; **59** AA/M Bonnet; **60** AA/M Bonnet; **61** AA/C Sawyer; **62** AA/C Sawyer; **63** AA/M Bonnet; **66l** AA/M Bonnet; **66c** AA/M Bonnet; **66r** AA/M Bonnet; **67l** AA/M Bonnet; **67r** AA/M Bonnet; **68l** AA/M Bonnet; **68/69t** AA/M Bonnet; **68/69b** AA/M Bonnet; **69t** AA/M Bonnet; **69b** AA/M Bonnet; **70l** AA/M Bonnet; **70/71t** AA/M Bonnet; **70br** AA/M Bonnet; **71bl** AA/M Bonnet; **71tr** AA/M Bonnet; **71br** AA/M Bonnet; **72l** AA/M Bonnet; **72tr** AA/M Bonnet; **72/73br** AA/M Bonnet; **73t** AA/M Bonnet; **73b** AA/M Bonnet; **74tl** AA/M Bonnet; **74/75t** AA/M Bonnet; **74bl** AA/M Bonnet; **74br** AA/M Bonnet; **75t** AA/M Bonnet; **75bl** AA/M Bonnet; **75br** AA/M Bonnet; **76l** AA/M Bonnet; **76c** AA/M Bonnet; **76r** AA/M Bonnet; **77l** AA/M Bonnet; **77r** AA/M Bonnet; **78** AA/M Bonnet; **79t** AA/M Bonnet; **79b** Josep Ferrer/Alamy; **80t** AA/M Bonnet; **80bl** AA/M Bonnet; **80br** AA/M Bonnet; **81t** AA/M Bonnet; **81b** vario images GmbH & Co.KG/Alamy; **82t** AA/M Bonnet; **83t** AA/M Bonnet; **84t** AA/M Bonnet; **85t** AA/C Sawyer; **86t** AA/C Sawyer; **87** AA/C Sawyer; **90l** AA/M Bonnet; **90tr** AA/M Bonnet; **90br** AA/M Bonnet; **91** AA/M Bonnet; **91bl** AA/M Bonnet; **91br** AA/M Bonnet; **92l** AA/M Bonnet; **92tr** AA/M Bonnet; **92br** AA/M Bonnet; **93t** AA/M Bonnet; **93bl** AA/M Bonnet; **93br** AA/M Bonnet; **94tl** AA/M Bonnet; **94bl** AA/M Bonnet; **94/95** AA/M Bonnet; **96/97** AA/M Bonnet; **97tr** Christopher Pillitz/Alamy; **97br** AA/M Bonnet; **98l** AA/M Bonnet; **98c** AA/M Bonnet; **98r** AA/M Bonnet; **99t** AA/M Bonnet; **99bl** AA/M Bonnet; **99br** AA/M Bonnet; **100t** AA/M Bonnet; **100b** AA/M Bonnet; **101** AA/M Bonnet; **102** AA/M Bonnet; **103** AA/M Bonnet; **104** AA/M Bonnet; **105** AA/C Sawyer; **106** AA/C Sawyer; **107** AA/M Bonnet; **108t** AA/C Sawyer; **108tc** AA/M Bonnet; **108c** AA/M Bonnet; **108bc** AA/M Bonnet; **108b** AA/M Bonnet; **109** AA/C Sawyer; **110** AA/C Sawyer; **111** AA/C Sawyer; **112** AA/C Sawyer; **113** AA/M Bonnet; **114** AA/M Bonnet; **115** AA/M Bonnet; **116** AA/M Bonnet; **117** AA/M Bonnet; **118** AA/M Bonnet; **119** AA/M Bonnet; **120t** AA/M Bonnet; **120l** European Central Bank; **121** AA/M Bonnet; **122t** AA/M Bonnet; **122b** AA/M Bonnet; **123t** AA/M Bonnet; **123bl** AA/M Bonnet; **123br** AA/S McBride; **124t** AA/M Bonnet; **124bl** AA/M Bonnet; **124bc** AA/M Bonnet; **124br** AA/M Bonnet; **125t** AA/M Bonnet; **125bl** AA; **125bc** AA; **125br** AA/M Bonnet.

Every effort has been made to trace the copyright holders, and we apologise in advance for any accidental errors. We would be happy to apply any corrections in the following edition of this publication.